Platinum Publishing

FATIMA OMAR KHAMISSA &
PLATINUM PUBLISHING

Present

Property Trendsetters

Successful Toronto Real Estate Experts
Share Key Insider Secrets

Platinum Publishing
c/o Fatima Omar Khamissa
18-3555 Don Mills Road
Suite 131
Toronto
Ontario
M2H 3N3

Liability Disclaimer

Like anything in life, there are no guarantees that using the methods mentioned by the publisher by any of the contributors will result in the same success mentioned.

Although the author and publisher have made every effort to ensure that the information in this book was correct at press time, the author and publisher do not assume and hereby disclaim any liability to any party for any loss, damage, or disruption caused by errors or omissions, whether such errors or omissions result from negligence, accident, or any other cause.

The information contained within this book is strictly for educational purposes. If you wish to apply ideas contained in this book, you are taking full responsibility for your actions.

This book is being provided to you with the understanding that the staff, contributors and author of this book have not created this book for the purpose of engaging in the rendering of legal, accounting, tax, financial planning, insurance or investment advice. On such matters, please consult your own personal legal, accounting, tax, financial planning, insurance or investment professional advisor. Due to the nature of ever changing tax laws and rates, all of the information have been prepared based on the laws in effect at the time the book was written.

ISBN: 978-0-9953136-8-2

You are about to meet real people,
With real strategies,
In a real world,
Making a real difference.

All profits from this book will be donated Nisa Homes to support and assist women fleeing violent abusive relationships. Nisa Homes educates them so they can re-invent themselves and create a prosperous new future for themselves and their children.

Table of Contents

PILLARS OF BUSINESS SUCCESS
Tim Syrianos

As owner and broker of record for RE/MAX Ultimate Realty, one of my core beliefs in life and in business is that "With us, you're not a number." This belief speaks to each and every realtor on our team, in the way we interact with the consumer and is, in essence, what I want to translate as an image within the industry.

To consistently practice this belief daily is important because it's the way I want all our clients to feel when dealing with our agents and firm. It's a core belief that we first foster within our support team, filtering through to our agents (as they are our clients also), with the ultimate purpose of it emanating to the consumer. After all, who has ever enjoyed feeling like a number? I know I haven't.

Take the Time to Listen

Taking the time to listen and being open minded, by believing that everyone meets for a reason and investing in learning about someone and what they want to accomplish is important. You may have met for today, for a purpose that won't be realized until next week, next month or even for 5 years from now. There Is definitely a reason why two people's paths have crossed.

This consistent small act of kindness, taking the time to meet and listen, has created for me a reputation within and outside the industry of authentic leadership and created valued relationships that created a stronger personal brand that has crossed provincial and country borders.

Reputation Matters in Business Success

To me, reputation matters more than anything and while I realistically know that as humans, it's natural that any one of us may not always do things right, doing the right thing is never wrong.

While there are many different ways people may measure success, in my opinion, one of the pillars of a successful person and business is the positive representation of our industry. This attracts success because people want to be around and work with reputable people. Within the entire organization, at every meeting and event, I always remind everyone that each and every person doesn't just represent themselves. Their work, their conduct and interaction, are a collective brand and reflection of each and every person. It starts from the way the first call is answered, the way someone who walks in is greeted, the quality of the marketing material and the complete results they experience with us. It's important to take nothing for granted and remember to work like you're constantly being interviewed with the lights and cameras always on!

This belief didn't just awaken within me overnight. I'll never forget some of the conversations I had with my parents and one of them that stuck in my mind was around reputation. As a young man, under the age of 20, just newly licensed in the real estate industry, I remember being called in to have a seat so we could talk about my business future. Handing me a copy of the telephone directory white pages (that was how we found people's numbers before Google), my father asked me to look up our last name.

At that moment I realized for the first time that we were the only family with our last name in the book. When I pointed to our name and stated this, he simply said, "Don't ever forget it and don't ever embarrass our name." He then continued to explain to me the merits of protecting our reputation. "If you can't do something, politely decline, shake their hand and tell the truth."

Multiply the effects by also being the only realtor with my last name in Toronto and you can feel the importance of his lesson and the emotions it created. This lesson was a blessing and I live by his words to this day. Money can come and go, but nothing is more important than reputation.

Today, you don't have to be the only one with a last name on Google for this principle to apply. This was further proven to me at a recent session we held within our office. It was a panel that consisted of many of our top performers. In the interview process, there was a character trait that was evident in all of their answers to my questions. While this may not be the case for every person in society, this group of successful real estate agents all cared about what others thought of them. They demonstrated servant leadership and their core belief was to place the needs of their client first. They acknowledged that a happy client brought them more success through the positive word of mouth reinforcement and referrals.

There was one specific quote that resonated with me that described them and the way they do business. "You need to do a hundred good things for one person to find out but only one for one hundred to find out." Powerful words to remind ourselves of daily with every consumer interaction. We now live in a world where platforms exist and quickly allow us to share our experiences. More than ever, consumers depend and believe reviews online. It is easy to reach thousands of people with a click of button. Reputation is paramount to future success!

Create Business Relationships
That are Consumer Focused

Another pillar of success is the important relationship that must be between a brokerage and its agents. There was a time where there were only 20-30 agents per office and the office controlled everything. However, the hiring process of an agent over the last 20 years is vastly different than what it used to be.

As margins to operate a brokerage continued to erode, and agents had more control, models within our industry become more focused on more agents, regardless of their individual possibilities for success. In the race to see how many bodies could be hired, oversight and accountability also diminished.

I am confident that this is not the future of a successful brokerage or agent. For one, the level of service can't be predictable and repeatable with that model. Secondly, the failure rate and the level of inexperience that consumers would witness could tarnish the industry. As courses become tougher and legislature is continuously being updated, the focus is (and should be) to protect the consumer and provide a better experience.

Traits of a Successful Brokerage-Realtor Partnership

A brokerage that is not based on the number of bodies hired, provides an environment of collaboration and learning, and treats the agent as a "business partner" will succeed. A successful agent of the future needs to focus on being part of an environment that cultivates their entrepreneurial spirit and fosters success. Successful brokerages create an environment that has a balance between an agent's autonomy and accountability to professionalism through constant investment into their career.

Our focus is the "business partner" approach. We make every effort to support, provide leadership and guidance while providing services to make day-to-day operations more efficient, affordable and create business by promoting our agents. As partners with our realtors, we focus on lead generation though any platform or media opportunity. This is a true partnership!

I whole-heartedly believe that you can teach anything and everything to anyone with the exception of ethics. There is no place within our brokerage and shouldn't be within the industry, where a person is allowed to operate in a way that is not reminiscent of the code of conduct and ethics required within the industry. While there will always be a place for many different business models, both virtual and brick and mortar, with a balance between both, the environment must also provide real life touch and is focused on building people.

Building People Leads to Building a Successful Business

My belief centers around the approach that we use to build people and people build successful businesses. Building people is a unique perspective in our industry. This entails focusing on people's habits, one's belief system, and the fears that are associated with failure and in some cases, the fear of success. For example, we might discover that what makes one happy is more money, or maybe someone else cares more about work-life balance. We look at things like why one person focuses on lost opportunities and takes no time to remember and take note of their successes and then we seek to teach our partners how to overcome these challenges.

Building people consists of creating a picture in the mind that energizes one to start the day and lose track of time because of the pure enjoyment of the tasks at hand. After all, unlocking passion and having fun is not "work." We believe in inspiring leadership by sharing a quote at the right time, lending an ear without speaking and role playing a scenario to provide real-life experience. These types of activities assist someone to unlock their potential. Having people in our organization that are open to coaching, mentoring, and paying it forward is how everyone grows together.

I was once asked to describe the inner workings of a successful real estate brokerage. What would I compare it to? How is it possible to cultivate a team environment when everyone is working to achieve their own goals? Is it every person for themselves? These are all interesting questions and I realized there is another environment that works similarly and it's in sports. It's like a baseball team.

Let's compare the similarities. Every baseball player is primarily focused on their own stats. They practice, drill and rehearse every aspect of their game, and when they take the field, they manage and focus on their own space and results. A baseball player could hit a bunt, a single, a double, a triple or even a home run. In real estate, this can be compared to the size of transaction one may be involved in.

In baseball, a player may swing and miss countless times and ultimately strike out. In real estate, an agent speaks to hundreds of prospective clients and only successfully works with a few. What separates the successful from the unsuccessful for either professional is just a few extra contacts (no pun intended). The fielding in the game is no different than the interaction between professionals working together to avoid bad outcomes and provide a smooth transaction. Pitching and catching may very well reflect negotiating in the business world, sometimes it's delivered slow, or best delivered with a direct, fast approach.

While the game is being played, the leadership of a baseball team is similar to the leadership of a brokerage. We both seek talent, coachable people, and great role models. We focus on cultivating untapped talent. We work daily on assisting our team on adjusting their approach, improving and being students of the work needed to be successful. We also both manage personalities, egos, on getting our team of individuals out of ruts and pushing them to believe in their God-given ability. So, while it may be thought of as an individual industry, the goal at the end of each year, is to help everyone grow and collectively win the championship.

Showing Values with Your Business Vision

The vision the leadership of our brokerage demonstrates to our realtors is to not fear competition, change and being open to opportunity. It's best not to only be taught with words, but to see values demonstrated through actions.

A couple of years ago, our lease was coming due at one of our locations. I knew that I didn't want to renew, and it was important to purchase a building. We already owned the real estate for all of our other locations, and I knew that with my present lease coming up for renewal, now was the time to make a move. So, I met with the landlord and expressed that I would be very interested in staying, but only if he sold me the building. When he turned me down, I provided him written notice that I will not be exercising the option to renew.

During our meeting, he really thought that we were meeting to negotiate an extension. He looked at me perplexed and questioned my sensibility since I only had 6 months remaining and didn't have a location to move to. He reminded me that he has a great location and he will lease it to another competing real estate firm within days.

I looked at him, smiled and said, "If I woke up every day worried about my competition, I wouldn't be in this business." He laughed and commented how he respected my courage. I simply told him, "That's the absolute truth." I wake up every day to provide the value of building people with confidence. That's invaluable!

Keep Your Eyes to the Future—Do Not Fear Change

Keeping your eyes to the future and not fearing change is probably one of the most important beliefs one must adopt, and I remind myself daily. Growing is not only measured in monetary terms. To me, it's always been more rewarding measuring personal growth than only looking at monetary growth.

I remember my difficult beginnings. No one ever sees those. They don't know about how my family came to Canada with a few bucks in their pocket with dream of a better life. They don't know of the struggles and how we all have them. They only see one's success and believe that it has always come easy when, in reality, there is difficulty every step of the way.

I remember being licensed during one of the most difficult financial times in Canadian history. The recession that began in 1989 and lasted through 1996. At that time, I was a young man struggling to figure out the business while witnessing plummeting house values, people losing their properties to foreclosure and interest rates continuing to rise to over 14%. Working through those challenging times provided insight and perspective that will last a lifetime.

Turning Points & Lessons Learned

There was one specific moment that was a turning point in my career that I want to share. It was September of 1993, I was still living at home and I remember sitting with my parents. I poured my heart out to them and provided every excuse about the shortcomings of the market and what was at fault with it for my lackluster success. But, this time, it was different. They'd had enough of the excuses. They looked at me and said "It's OK that this type of work and business isn't for you. You're not a failure. Maybe it's time you go back to school for something different." I was shocked and I couldn't believe they said that to me. But, what played out in my mind and came out in words is what surprised me more. I looked at them and said, "Give me 6 months and if I don't make it, I will leave the real estate industry."

That was my cannon announcement to the universe. I refused to fail and knew that I would do everything possible not to. I immediately wanted to change my environment, so I joined RE/MAX as I wanted to be surrounded by like-minded professionals. In one of the worst markets in Canadian history, I helped more families move in 6 months than I had in the past 4 years. It made me realize that focusing on the problem is not the way to find a solution. Opportunity lies within, between or beside every challenge. It's up to us to relax, take a breath and allow it to appear. And when it does, to apply it as soon as possible.

That time of personal growth through experiences is what catapulted me to take risks and believe in the greater purpose of building people. The mind shift I made was to focus on helping families grow through home ownership. I always believed in real estate and that I was the right person to help everyone.

As my career grew, I continued to evolve and I remember feeling even more fulfilled coaching, training, and creating business for my team. It was more fun witnessing their successes than just working on my own. It felt effortless and this triggered me to explore something within the same business, but different. I knew it was time to explore helping agents grow.

I convinced the owner of the brokerage I was part of that I was the right successor to her business and bought the company. However, it's easy to second guess your decision when you are suddenly becoming a non-selling broker and leaving a sales career behind (which is all you've ever known) and surrendering your autonomy.

It was a couple days before the announcement, and I had just finished signing the closing documents that contained every guarantee imaginable. While I knew it was right, my nerves still held tight. So much so that on the eve of making the announcement, I started to lose my voice. Luckily, my wife came to the rescue with a card that I will always cherish, the card read, "Don't be afraid of change, be afraid of not changing." Could there be a more fitting statement for life growth?

Don't be Afraid of Change—Be Afraid of not Changing!

Over the last 30 years in the industry, I have witnessed a lot of change. Our industry used to be focused on "Consumer, Agent, House" and today it's "Consumer, House, Agent," in that order. There are start-ups and companies daily that want to change our industry. Many call them disruptors. I am a big believer that the word "disrupters" when looked at internally should be removed from a business owner's mindset and vocabulary. I don't believe industries should categorize and confuse positive change, doing something better or easier as being "disruptors." In my opinion, this term is used by industries and inadvertently creates a protectionist feeling of how their personal business will change for the worse, whenever change comes along.

Today we embrace services like Uber, Skip the Dishes, Airbnb, and VRBO. Yet, if you were in the taxi industry or hotel business, these services suddenly become a perceived threat to the way you've always done business and some even take action to not let them join the industry. In reality, we forget that we're also consumers and need to constantly think like consumers when providing services. We shouldn't anger or frustrate them. Instead, we must continuously embrace changes and ask ourselves not only how we can make it easier, but also what opportunity exists within this change.

We must remember that consumers tell all businesses where to go twice. Once, where to go to help find them and assist them and the second time, where to go if we don't listen. I bet you would do the same thing if you were greeted with roadblocks.

We will continue to exist in a fast-paced, ever-changing environment where the internet and platforms of tomorrow will provide the power of information not just with clicks but voice commands as well. It will continuously change our expectations and acknowledge that it's a societal shift in how we must interact with the consumer of tomorrow. Our value is in interpreting data, understanding, and explaining how market trends affect the consumer, and ultimately guiding the client to make the best decision possible.

The real estate agent in our brokerage is always reminded of the positives of why they entered the business. With us, no one is a number. We are focused on taking the time to listen and in assisting people in achieving their goals of property ownership. We believe in building a reputation by representing the industry proudly, being present, being a great role model and a team player. We provide advice that is in the best interest of the client. We are business partners and continuously invest in the success of our realtors. We never fear change as within change lies opportunity. We teach our partners to differentiate and not accept "how it's always been done" and to seek ways to do things better. Because of the pillars of success that we teach our partners and structure our entire business around, we will build people into the best version of themselves and help consumers realize their dreams of property ownership.

ABOUT THE AUTHOR

Since entering real estate in 1989, young and ambitious, Tim Syrianos continuously strove to take in and learn as much as possible about his chosen industry which led to extensive knowledge in all aspects of real estate. Along the way, his dedication and efforts also did not go unnoticed as Tim became the recipient of numerous achievement awards as awarded by RE/MAX International. His knowledge and expertise have been sought after as an industry speaker and he has been featured in numerous media interviews including newspaper, radio (CFRB "Ask the Experts") and TV (CP24, CBC, CFTO, CTV, Omni and Global).

With the support of his wife and three children, he has focused his sights on helping realtors achieve success by mentoring and coaching his entire sales and support staff and sharing the knowledge necessary for success in the ever-changing real estate industry. Tim has the reputation of a visionary when it comes to recognizing industry trends and embracing technology. He deeply believes that one should not be afraid of change and instead should be afraid of not changing.

Tim has also served as part of the TREB Board of Directors from 2012-2019, as Board of Director with the Ontario Real Estate Association and as the 2017/2018 President of the Toronto Real Estate Board—the largest real estate board in the world. Tim is determined to fulfill his dream of building a brokerage surrounded by the best, most reputable realtors in Greater Toronto that will deliver the level of service and experience clients deserve and expect. Through Tim's leadership, RE/MAX Ultimate Realty Inc., brokerage has built an enviable reputation in Toronto as the "go to" brokerage for clients and realtors.

Notes: ✍

Notes:

THE VALUE OF A STAGED HOME
Carolynn Tersigni

Since 1972 the real estate industry saw a new profession emerge that would help make your home stand out, sell faster and bring you more money. Some called it house fluffing at first. Fast forward and with a peak into the psychology of staging we see that it is more than just moving furniture around and organizing clutter. As a professionally Certified Home Stager I have become the link between the real estate agent, the seller and the buyer. I am the professional that understands what features to highlight, which to minimize and how to create a beautiful, balanced space that is easy to emotionally connect with.

I feel like I should admit that I am quite unique in my field. With a background of Design and Holistic Medicine, my superpower is this combination that makes my work unique over most stagers. I not only understand the design principles of function but I also understand the psychology of how we are influenced by energy.

My career has evolved from a background that came from interior design to alternative natural medicine. Over the last 20 years my work has come full circle to incorporate both of my backgrounds. Always eager to learn I came to understand the connection we have to our spaces. I love that I see a space and instantly can see it transformed in my head, whether it's a room or the whole house, staying there or moving from it.

My work includes:

- Redesigning a space to look and function better

- Staging homes, condos or new builds for developers

- New move set up

- Feng Shui balancing for homes and businesses

- Detecting and clearing energy imbalances in homes, businesses and land

- Lifestyle Design and Coaching

Before the internet and virtual home tours were put to music, sellers could just clean up the yard, wash the windows and dust the floors before putting a FOR SALE sign in the yard. But the market has greatly changed. Much of the point of staging is to not only create an attractive space for the viewings but perhaps even more importantly to create a beautiful video and photos that publicize the property on the internet. It has become the way people judge whether they will even want to physically see the home. It has become the filter. We all know what the camera is capable of doing to ourselves in pictures and videos. Imagine the cluttered, crazy coloured, over furnished home in a video and photo. Not a pretty sight and definitely not an asset to selling the property. Since it has become part of the process to selling a property, it has now made those who do not use staging the home the one that stands out in the listings, and not in a good way. With our world changing it may change the way people buy homes as well. The value of staging a home will be even higher knowing that the only way people may get to see homes may be from the virtual tours and photos online. The open house concept may be a thing of the past. There have been many homes I have staged in the past that sold strictly from the online photos.

Think of how our brains are trained to spot the imperfections within ourselves and others. We remember the crazy sweater worn to an event just as much as we remember the crazy purple drapes in the bedroom of a home we went to see. Something will stick in our mind which we will use to recall it later on. That is where I come in. From a neutral point of view I can spot and modify those crazy purple drapes and change the focus to the beautiful fireplace or bay window instead. Accentuating the positive.

My job is to make you remember only the positive attributes and to give you the opportunity to emotionally connect with the home. People shopping for their home will always see quite a few homes. What do you want them to remember about your home when they are recalling what they saw?

Everyone believes their home is beautiful, works well and that everyone would want it. Everyone's perception comes from only their view though. If our homes are typically cluttered and in need of repair even that will still be perceived as perfect in our view until the day it needs to be listed for sale. Then suddenly living that way is not appropriate. The real estate agent comes to see the home and tries to politely say what needs to be changed to help the sale. I become part of the agent's team that is responsible for graciously doing that talk with the home owner. Their focus is to get your listing agreement signed, not pointing out that the purple drapes need to go. I am usually called in to give a very detailed assessment of what needs to be done from the entire property prior to the listing being put on the market. Once I have been asked to help with the staging I begin to create a plan. A staging plan outlines where you put your time, effort and money for the best return on investment. Too many people think of staging as a process that costs money. Consider the money you spend to get your home ready for sale as a necessary investment. The cost of staging will always bring you far more money on the sale price. So much so it is one of the fastest ways to increase your investment. Clients are always happy and surprised to realize that within a few days or weeks they have made a 300% increase on their staging investment.

For me the house becomes a canvas from which I will enhance the best attributes of that home. I eliminate the stress for the family and even for the agent who now knows the house will be ready by the agreed date. I have been seen painting, cleaning flower beds and even packing the house up all to help the home owner and agent Utilizing what furniture and décor the family already has I will add my own collections to enhance or I will coordinate furniture rental for the empty or new build scenarios. The home owner does not need to purchase furniture or décor accents. Neither does the real estate agent. I believe real estate agents should use their specialty knowledge to sell homes and should probably not try to be the specialist in staging it as well. Often they can be seen buying shopping carts of décor at Home Sense stores to add to a client's home thinking that is staging. Not only is it unethical to use it for a job and then return it to the store when they have sold the house, but they are not doing their client any favours. With the home being for most people their largest investment, it deserves to have the best attention possible to net the largest return. The first impression can only be done once, make it count. The cost of staging will always be cheaper than if you and your agent decide to drop the price. For years I have been building my décor and furniture collections that keep up with the trends. I have plenty of inventory to stage many homes at a time. The easy part for the homeowner is that it is rented from me at a fraction of the cost compared to buying things you may not use at your new home. I carry a multitude of styles, colours and sizes to work with any home, condo or new build. Once the property sells the items are removed and cleaned to be ready for the next home. Stress free and easy.

Benefits of Staging for Sellers

- Staged properties attract more potential buyers

- With the house properly ready for sale, agents are more impressed and are able to support a higher list price.

- Homeowner doesn't need to purchase anything that they may not use again.

- Sellers have less stress knowing the house sells faster and for more money

- Staging provides less packing to be done before the move.

- De-cluttering and organizing allows for faster closings.

- Staging is typically done in one day, even while you are at work.

I get such joy working with a family through the selling process that when they ask me to help them design and decorate their new home, I know that I really connected with them. To me that is a compliment that I appreciate. I once had a client that really needed help with her home. She had to sell quickly. After my initial visit to the home we came up with a plan and budget. Three days later I arrived and spent the day transforming her home. When she arrived home after work she was stunned to see her home. She did not recognize it. She fell back in love with her home. It looked fresh and inviting. That was a Tuesday. By that Saturday the house was full of people coming to see it. She had intended to have it open the Sunday as well. After a multitude of offers she decided with her agent to accept an offer that was nearly $60,000. 00 over her asking price. I was so happy for her. I was so grateful that she asked me to duplicate what I had created there in her new home. She loved the look and feel I had created and knew she couldn't duplicate it on her own. Only 10% of the population really have an eye for seeing things done before they really are. I appreciate that I have a keen eye for visualizing. I am able to take those ideas people see in magazines and on TV and can create those ideas for them.

Benefits for the Real Estate agent

- Working with a stager provides an objective third party opinion. The stager will create the space that can easily be marketed

- Staged properties always look better online and in print. Size and perspective are always more accurate. An empty room does not show well.

- Staged properties help grow the agent's business. Satisfied buyers and sellers will refer more.

- Staging tells buyers and sellers that the agent markets their listings well.

- A seller who has invested time to ready the property are more likely to appreciate the work an agent does to market and sell it.

- The agent knows that closings can be faster and with less issues.

Once you decide to list your home it goes from a home to a house really. The emotional attachments need to start unplugging. How many times have you been to a home only to be distracted by the adorable baby picture or the trophy that someone earned on the mantle? Those are emotional attachments to the owner and the home. It becomes difficult and a major distraction to view a home and what someone remembers most about the home is the adorable baby pictures everywhere. The potential buyers only see you there and cannot visualize themselves in the home. De-personalizing also helps protect the family of revealing too much information. Names on trophies and pictures of your children do not need to be seen by those coming to see the home or online. My 19 page assessment outlines the importance of why and how we unplug (neutralize) your home.

Today's buyers want move in ready homes most of them. They also can be very impatient. They want to close the sale on Friday, move in on Saturday, meet the neighbours on

Sunday and have the kids in school and be back to work on Monday. Staged homes really help everyone involved, the seller, agent and buyer.

Benefits for the Buyers

- They can easily see what they are buying

- They can emotionally connect with the home, visualizing themselves there.

- A professionally staged home shows the buyers how their furniture can fit effectively.

- Buyers have peace of mind knowing that all the repairs and updating are done.

- They can move in and get into their routine of life faster.

- Staging gives ideas to the buyer how to decorate

When staging a house, I need to appeal to all 5 senses to create that balanced feeling. As a Stager with my unique approach, part of my magic is that I follow the Feng Shui principles in each property I work on. This is done discreetly and effectively. It is more about balancing the senses, elements, colors and energy flow. Not about placing the typical Feng Shui symbols everywhere. What does the energy flow have to do with selling your home? Let's imagine that everything is energy and all that has ever happened in our homes has left something behind. The great moments as much as the arguments, illness, deaths, divorces, job stress etc. have all been energetically recorded in your home. Year after year building up. The homes baggage becomes heavy and our positive emotional connection becomes more and more difficult to feel. That initial emotional connection we had when we found and bought the home becomes a distant memory.

As a very energy perceptive person I can easily see and feel that heavy energy we often live with. I am able to clear that heaviness through what I call Energy Prepping for those not selling their home as much as for those that are. Think of it as scrubbing clean all the layers of emotional layers that have built up year after year. As our society has become more energy conscious, my work of Feng Shui and Energy Prepping spaces has become widely accepted and sought after. I appreciate that I am able to help families and businesses clean that energetic slate whenever they need it.

As we have become more accepting of how energy has an impact on our lives, people shopping for their next dream home will expect that the cords of attachment (emotional layers) will have been cleared. A true emotional connection will be more accurate for the new family. A clean slate allows the new family to create their own energy imprint on their home. Quite often people share stories that they never really were able to connect with some of their homes in the past. There was a feeling that they could not put into words other than that things went downhill from when they moved in. Relationships, health or money changes are the first to appear. Understanding how energy is recorded in our spaces purchasing a home from a family going through a divorce for example, it is easy to see how that could affect the next family living there if the energy isn't cleaned up.

As our society has been changing dramatically this year, the need to energetically clean our homes and businesses is more important than ever. Energy smudging is one of the quickest ways to reset the energy in a space.

Feng Shui and staging compliment themselves in so many ways. The most notable aspects of staging also stem from creating the harmony using Feng Shui. Colour, lighting, clutter clearing, good working order, a balance of nature inside and clear flowing energy should all be activated in a home whether selling or not.

Have you ever noticed how colour affects your mood? Colours evoke emotion. Quite often in listings I see over and over again the same colour used as an accent in every house. Red means STOP in our minds eye, but also symbolizes fire and anger. Somehow some stagers were told to use red to make an impact. Without understanding the value colours have, distributing the wrong colour symbol throughout our home for sale can have a negative impact. Our eyes naturally connect similar colors together. It is very important that a suitable accent colour is used throughout the staging that fits the style of the home and allows the eyes to follow it throughout the rooms to connect them. Then there is the issue with those homes that have the bright orange wall in the family room that can be seen from the front door. It probably was lovely when the family put it there but for some buyers they struggle to see past it, even though it is only paint. In my assessments I have appropriate colour selections that can neutralize and harmonize any room.

Staging is not the same as decorating a home. There needs to be a balance of nature, colour and furniture but only enough to showcase the space and show the rooms purpose. If the listing says there are 4 bedrooms they should be staged as 4 bedrooms, not an office, junk room or gym. People are looking to see if their king size bed will fit into the master (or principle) bedroom. Remember visualizing can be a challenge for some.

If buyers can connect with your space and can see or feel themselves living there, then I have successfully helped one family finish their lesson and the new family can begin theirs. Once I create a space that is balanced, decluttered, de-personalized and feels inviting, then it is ready for its new family to find and connect with it.

Why is Feng Shui so Important?

If you knew that your home was a visual representation of all that you are, would you look at it the same way? Would you still leave things perhaps all over, cluttering areas, having things in need of repair?

Feng Shui is by no means a new concept that was created to complicate our lives and cause us to spend money chasing a better feeling. It is an ancient system that translates to mean wind and water. Two elements that feed everything on this planet. Every culture uses the principles of Feng Shui regardless of what they call it. It is not based on religion which is why it is used all over the world. It is based on the balance of elements that influence all of us whether we want to believe that or not. Since everything is vibrating at a frequency that allows it to be seen and felt, the spaces in our lives record everything that happens. Our home is a living reflection of us and what our lessons are.

We chose our homes based on the lessons we are striving to learn. For most people they would think they chose their home because of its proximity to work or the kid's school or because they got a great price for it etc. When we get those urges to move or even renovate our homes, often it is because we have learned the lesson that space has provided.

Feng Shui is really a large umbrella that trains us to include energy, geomancy, astrology, numerology, clutter clearing, interior design, colour theory and an understanding of the elements. Living in an environment without the balance of nature slowly reduces our life force. Our home is meant to be our safe- haven; a place where our soul is nurtured. Your home is very much alive and listening to you. Feng Shui won't solve or prevent every problem in your life, but when you acknowledge and respect it, it will always show you where you are on your journey and remind you of what is important. It's like that friend that has your best interests at heart.

My work as a Feng Shui specialist is to simplify your life so you can easily achieve what you set out to do. Regardless if it is that you need to sell your home, have better relationships, more money, better health or on the deeper level you are seeking to have that place of peace to retreat to at the end of your day. I am the coach of your team that wants to make sure all the players are represented on your team (your elements are healthy and equally represented). I am the one who will check to make sure the symbols you have in your space speak accurately of the life you want. I am not standing in your life or forest as the saying goes, so I can easily notice and point out the symbols that are sending out mixed signals to your life plan. Remember energy goes where attention goes. You should never operate from a place of fear using Feng Shui. It is merely a system that works with your intuition to align your inner life to your external view of life. Once they are in alignment we are content, have more energy for the joys of our life, are healthy and wealthier and feel like we can contribute to the world. We are not here to just exist. We are here to thrive and expand.

If we take the time to listen to a person's story we realize that everyone has a varied past that creates their puzzle of life. Mine is no different. People might say that I am on a mission to learn and be of service. I would agree and from my view, every experience has brought me to where I am now. Everything fits together in my puzzle whether I love all the pieces or not. There are no pieces that don't have a place. From the numerous courses I have studied, the personal growth from working in networking companies to having the courage to do what I love, I appreciate what my puzzle looks like. Even if at the time I couldn't see how everything would come together, I still trusted that it would. I have come full circle to discover that I can combine my design abilities with my training as a Holistic Practitioner. My love of design and natural medicine created a career that is very rewarding. Of all the modalities I have studied when I got to studying how we live with the programs given to us from our environment, I was hooked. Somehow I have always known that everything is connected. Perhaps my numerology skills confirmed that for me. Regardless seeing the links to nature, the animals we notice, how we react to situations and how we live in our homes it all became very clear how much they had an impact on our life. If we listen to our intuition we all have that feeling that happens when things are in balance. That is the feeling using Feng Shui brings us. That sense that our space is a reflection of our authentic self, not what the magazines suggest for the next trend that lasts 6 months. Decorating a home is usually not done by the entire family living in it. Often one person takes on the task to get it done. Sometimes they go online to get ideas or they hire someone to help them. If we know that the home is a visual representation of our thoughts, feelings and lessons shouldn't everyone be represented and be part of the decorating process? Working with a Feng Shui expert will ensure that the home represents everyone living there and is balanced for all.

When you hear the word Feng Shui what is the first thing that pops into your head? Do you think you can't use it because you are not Chinese or that you already have a religion? Who are the people that are attracted to Feng Shui in today's world? From what I have seen over the years, they are the people that know something is off but can't quite put their finger on it. Perhaps it appears that their luck has changed, they've lost a job, had an illness, relationships have become strained or they don't enjoy being at home. Sometimes it happens right after moving into the home. Sometimes it comes when someone leaves the home because of passing away or going away to school. I believe we chose our homes based on the lessons we are striving to learn. For most people they would think they chose their home because of its proximity to work or the kids school or because they got a great price for it etc. In reality though, we chose it from our subconscious mind that knows what we want to learn to grow our soul. That is why when we get those urges to move or even renovate our homes, often it is because we have learned the lesson that space has provided. We are trying to create the environment that our soul is looking for. The style of Feng Shui I studied and resonate with comes from acknowledging how important our intuition is. The practice of being mindful whether we learn it through yoga, meditation, journaling, art or just observing, it always brings us to the point when we see the connection we have to everything. We are not separate from the world. We are all one, whether we want to be or not. Often in the homes I go to help, the people don't see the connection the dirty laundry on the floor represents to their relationships or that the broken stove represents challenges in the prosperity of the family. The symbols in our home get translated to our soul. A visual so we can better see what areas we need help.

I don't believe we intentionally chose symbols that have a negative meaning to have in our home. Sometimes we are gifted things that don't resonate well with us and we use them because we feel obligated. Have you ever been gifted with something for your home that you only put out when that person comes over? Maybe you leave it out only to think the negative thought every time you pass by it? Unintentional of course. That does not create a sanctuary. Often when I come to meet with a family those are the pieces they want to remove first, regardless if they are selling or staying.

 Some years back I went to help a family that had challenges with keeping the family together. Upon arriving at the home I noticed there were statues of women left near the curb in front of their home. They were just randomly standing on the grass. They were small statues, ones you often see in flower gardens. After speaking with the Mom I came to understand that the Mom (recently divorced) and the 2 daughters were having challenges staying together. The dining room was still in boxes from the move that had happened many months before. The symbols explained everything to me. It was my task to shine light on what they meant to the family. Sometimes it takes a different set of eyes to see the meanings. Knowing that everything is energy we need to realize how the universal symbols affect us. Seeing the statues at the curb looked like the daughters who were anxious to be out the house. Each one waiting for the opportunity to leave. The dining room which nurtures the family time together, was not created being that everything was still in boxes. The house never got unpacked because the 3 of them didn't feel connected in that house. It was a temporary place that they all wanted to leave. The emotions of the divorce and its impacts on all of them were never really addressed. We managed to create a remedy plan that connected the 3 of them together in that home, acknowledging the lessons it was providing. They were stronger together and were able to move their lives forward again.

The style of Feng Shui I use is one that uses crystals to help shift and hold energy in spaces. I find in North America we are very blessed with amazing natural crystals and we respect their beauty. If our culture taught us to use the typical Feng Shui symbols that is great, but for most who are opening up to using Feng Shui they don't have that connection. By using crystal remedies I find that people will appreciate the beauty of the crystal even if they don't remember why I put it there. If every time they see the crystal they think a positive thought, it has then served its purpose. Their mindfulness has begun.

Himalayan salt has always been a part of my work. I resonated with it as easily as I did to crystals. Knowing that Feng Shui is all about balancing the elements within us and our homes, using things from nature inside our homes is a natural fit. More plants, flowers, shells, crystals, salt and lights all help to shift and hold that feeling we seek in our homes and even businesses. With how busy our lives have become and how little we get to be in nature, it is vital that inside our homes we create that kind of space. With the natural energy that comes from crystals, salt, plants etc. they have the ability to neutralize the harm we have brought into our homes by having everything electronically connected. The electro-magnetic field (EMF) that we live with from our cell phones, computers, TV's and everything plugged in has a direct impact on our health. From immune diseases to fertility issues, links come back to the EMF world we have created. Our best solutions come from nature.

What about the earth energies that we did not create? In Europe you can hear stories of how the farmers watch their land before they develop it. They pay attention to where the animals stay, the condition of the vegetation and if insects like to congregate. What are they really looking at? Think of the earth as a representation of us. We have more similarities than most people realize. These wise farmers are reading the earth energies that are below the surface. Water streams and reservoirs, electrical currents and minerals all express themselves to the surface. Much like the eczema, acne and pigments that afflict us on our skin. Everything comes to the surface to show us what needs help.

The challenge for us comes when we build our homes and business on top of these energies. The farmers will watch their land for a year to understand if or where these earth energies run. Knowing this they can build their homes and barns in a stress- free zone that will benefit everyone that ever lives there. In North America we are not as diligent or patient in waiting to develop land for our use. Money seems to dictate the level of patience. These sources of earth energy have been associated with compromising our immune system when we spend time living on them. I have been trained to detect where these lines sometimes are on our properties. Not all properties have them running through them. But would you not want to know? My full circle came to me when I realized as a health practitioner I had lots of tools in my toolbox to help the person but if the environment they lived in had issues it had a one step forward, two steps back effect. Everything in our own world has an impact on our life.

There are signs that can indicate you may have some earth energies on your property. They are visible in unique ways. The sign looks like the cracks in your driveway, foundation or sidewalk that return even after repairs. They appear when you have bees that like to build and rebuild their nests on your back porch despite how many times you get rid of them. They appear with that dead tree in your yard that every time you replace it the next one dies as well. Maybe your cat likes to sit in the same area every day, whichever floor they are on. Same spot different floor. With our busy life we often don't put these connections together. We replace or repair over and over not noticing the pattern. My job is to detect if and what type of earth energy may be present on your property and remedy the area to make it healthy for its owners or buyers. Unfortunately, I cannot dig up the swatch of energy and move it. They can be several feet wide and deeper than we realize. That would not make our neighbours very happy with us. My work is to determine if you have areas that can affect you by sleeping on it, sitting at your desk, sofa or kitchen table. Places where we spend more time in our homes. We can clock many hours of our life on the sofa or in bed. It has an impact on our immune system over time. It is that silent visitor that brings to us the headaches that are consistent, the fatigue, the challenges sleeping and the relationship issues to name a few. I believe knowledge is power. By mapping your property I will give you the knowledge to use your property in the healthiest way possible. I never imagined when in high school my geography teacher said I should make maps, what he meant. I loved that course. If Mr. Clark could see me now. In an unconventional way I discovered how to map our land. Living in the ebb and flow of life is that peace we are all seeking. Everything has its place and purpose. We are the ones that decided where and how we would live on this planet. We need to listen to the clues the earth gives us about how to create the peace and balance we seek.

I like to simplify knowledge for people. Much of what I have studied, I can teach to empower others without packaging it in fear. I have studied many, many modalities over the years and I am still learning. I have created over the years 6 centers that were all about teaching and empowering others. If you are living in your space and you don't absolutely love being there, then perhaps that is a reason to bring me in. With a visit to your home or business and a discovery process we will make a plan to either stage for sale or create the sanctuary, abundance, health and relationships you have always wanted.

To help you get started here are some aspects that should be paid attention to if you are planning to stay in your home.

- Clear the clutter in your spaces, every floor, and every closet.

- Keep the front door of your home clear and use it regularly.

- Allow the chi energy to flow through your space

- Keep everything in good working order

- Get your home checked for geopathic stress (negative earth energies)

- Be mindful of the symbols and images in your home and what they represent.

- Create a sanctuary in your bedroom

- Use your kitchen to generate the loving energy of your home.

- Use nature symbols in your home to connect the indoors to the outdoors

ABOUT THE AUTHOR

Most of my business covers easily the GTA, but if there is someone I can help, location is not an issue. I also have created a beautiful Lifestyle Design Centre in Woodbridge, Ontario. There you will find crystals, home décor, unique Himalayan Salt Walls and much more. It is all part of my toolbox open for you to enjoy. I carry a large variety of crystals that can assist many challenges. There are many ways to accomplish what we want in life. Sharing knowledge is always in style. If I can ever help to answer a design, staging or health question please reach out. Public speaking at events is always an exciting way to share what I have learned and I have many topics to choose from.

I always appreciate referrals and honour them with my CTD Referral Program.

My Design centre is open by appointment to ensure personalized service.

Look for me on YouTube for helpful lifestyle videos.

Wishing you an abundant and healthy life that you deserve!

Carolynn Tersigni Lifestyle Design
250 Vaughan Valley Blvd. unit 250
Woodbridge, ON L4H 3C3
647-534-9252 text or call
Email: carolynntersigni@gmail.com
WEBSITE: Lifestyle2Design.com

Notes:

Notes: ✍

THE PATH OF ENTREPRENEURSHIP:
Mastering Action, Failure, Learning, Experiencing, Fixing and Redoing

Sina Dejnabadi

Sina Dejnabadi is a serial entrepreneur, an industrial engineer as well as a certified import and export specialist in Canada. He is also certified by CITP and FIBP. Sina is an elite member of Forum for Canada's International Trade Training known as FITT and a qualified expert in interior design and decoration as well as an NLP and Timeline Therapy Practitioner.

Sina is the President and CEO of Samia Canada, Inc., known as the "#1 company in supplying honeycomb construction panels." Sina also owns an e-commerce, online retail, social media and digital marketing agency called Samicore. Moreover, Sina is the founder of a coaching platform named First Class Seat Coaching.

Samia Canada, Inc. was established in 2010.

Honeycomb panels became industrialized in 1943. Primary aluminum bonding technology was applied to aircraft construction, generating metal bonding technology. In the early 1950's, Americans discovered a cement sandwich-structure, which is often called the "sandwich" formation, and applied to aircraft structures. In 1956, Americans made panels with an aluminum honeycomb sandwich structure. F-111 and F-14 fights jets use this structure to strengthen the plane's surface.

The technical characteristics of Samia Canada's products attract a wide range of industries from oil, gas, and aviation uses, to transportation, as well as architecture and in the construction industry. Samia Canada Inc. helps architects and designers benefit from the extraordinary "weight to strength" ratio that honeycomb panels provide. The initial idea of using hexagonal cells came from bees building their honeycomb in the nature.

The hexagonal shape reduces the cladding structure's weight and increase the capacity which results in lower costs, more durability, faster installation, a modern visual look and environmental sustainability.

Although Samia Canada generally focuses on providing materials for specific industries, they do receive requests for a variety of applications in different industries which include requests to meet the needs of Designers, Fabricators, and Installers.

Their products have been used in:

- Shipbuilding,
- Vacation RVs,
- Laser machines,
- Jet interiors,
- Subway cars,
- Elevators and escalators,
- Interior walls,
- Partitions,
- Doors,
- Floors,
- Ceilings, etc.

In the building industry, Samia Canada has helped architects, engineers, fabricators and installers utilizing the panels as cladding systems—either as a finished product or as a substrate in interior or exterior wall surfaces, floors, partitions, doors and building facades.

About Sina Dejnabadi, CEO of Samia Canada, Inc.

I started working at the age of 18. I earned a bachelor's degree in Industrial Engineering in Iran. Studying and working after high school gave me the chance to experience high profile businesses in my 20's. I started work as a Computer Operator and in Maintenance and within 2 years, I was promoted to Quality Assurance Manager. My company became one of the ten first ISO 9001 certified service companies as the local office for blue-chip companies like General Electric and Bosch in 2000.

In 2004 I started working in the oil and gas industry focused on the design, procurement and sales of equipment and systems to refineries, petrochemical plants, oil and gas pipelines and storage tank farms.

At the age of 26, I had the opportunity to work directly with well-known companies from UK, Canada, Italy, Germany, Spain, Australia and South Korea. Selling more than $85 million US within 5 years. I travelled extensively, completing more than 50 business trips visiting factories and procuring products in different countries. I was very passionate about my work.

In 2009 I moved to Canada. It was a great time for me to leave Iran since the sanction on oil and gas pushed the European and US based companies out of the country. I wanted to explore the world and stay in the international trade environment. Therefore, immigrating to Canada gave me that possibility.

However, there was a problem I had to sort out before completely detaching from my business in Iran. I had started a project in a refinery and had to finish it due to the security bonds we had in the project. We were manufacturing storage tank equipment for a huge oil depot and the Turkish supplier had delayed providing the material. I travelled to Istanbul more than 10 times to push them to finish the job without success. It was a very painful and ended up being the biggest business loss in my life. Our company paid an extra $150,000 to close this deal. We also paid double the tax because the Turkish company refused to submit the invoices.

This hassle became the best event in my professional life. During one of the stressful meetings in Turkey, I saw a piece of panel on the conference table that caught my attention. I stopped the other person while he was talking and asked him, "What is this?"

He said, "It's honeycomb panel."

I took it. I expected it to be much heavier and I realized how light it is. Then I asked about the usage.

"It's for the floating roof tanks due to strength and weight and also resistance against corrosion," he replied.

I closed my eyes and imagined where it could be used, reminding myself of all my visits to job sites and factories. I said "wow" in my heart without showing my excitement to the other person.

I asked if I could have a piece of that panel for myself. He agreed and gave a piece to me. I still have that piece as a symbol of my biggest loss that turned into my biggest income ever.

When I came to Canada, I intended to follow the oil and gas industry but shortly found the Canadian market different in many aspects. The oil and gas industry is concentrated in Alberta and I had to move to Calgary or Edmonton. I had great offers from reputed companies, but I wanted to open my own personal business.

It took me 3 days to sit and think deeply about my business with the piece of honeycomb as a fresh Canadian company in a competitive North American market.

Although the USA has been the centre of all Research & Development for design and application of honeycomb panels for the past 50 years, very few industries have a proper knowledge about this product. Aviation and military were the center of attention for honeycomb technology and patents were all around to protect this product from being distributed in other areas. Canada and civil applications were totally unfamiliar with this product and the significant features and advantages of this material.

Another limitation was accepted alloys of metals like aluminum for the aviation industry that could become very expensive for the other industries like construction compared with the other alternatives.

The number-one obstacle was the lack of knowledge about the product usage, and the advantages it could offer in different projects. Many standards and codes reflected traditional material in technical specifications. Architects use materials they know, what is on their accepted list of materials and also classic designs using traditional choices.

Weight and strength were two considerations that designers were thinking of. They desired a good ratio of weight to strength – achieved by testing a variety of materials; however, few people looked at honeycomb as a sandwich panel that can provide the best ratio.

In addition, there was a myth that rigidity, compression and fire resistance are provided by materials which have a metal base and are heavy. This principle was flawed. It resulted in using more raw materials, reduced capacities in applications and creates high labour costs for shipping, transportation and installations.

I knew I had something priceless in my hand. Years of experience with big corporations, knowledge about quality standards, my experience in international trade, my engineering background and my passion regarding Honeycomb panels assisted me in testing my product with a few customers.

We came up with new ideas. I did hundreds of lunch-and-learns and meetings with architects, designers, engineers and industrialists. I provided them with samples, shared our ideas and explained the advantages of my product.

Although that was the beginning of my own company entering into a completely new market, I invested a lot of money on trips and meetings. I also worked shoulder to shoulder with our potential customers and clients.

We had modern building materials as well, like thin porcelain slabs, stainless-steel decorative plates, and composites that could be used on large buildings to provide a modern look and make the building look lighter. However, there was a big risk to the contractors. Thin means there was a chance of breaking and consequently more equipment and workforce were needed to move the pieces. Attaching the product to the building was another challenge. Our product could solve many of these challenges by providing a flat substrate, attaching it to the structure through a profile system and most importantly strengthening the finishing lamination for installation and maintenance.

For many applications, like elevator cabs, the fabricators loved the product because they could reduce the engine and cables needed to offer the same weight capacity, at a more competitive price.

Stone companies have a chance of using thinner stone veneer, while easily moving big panels using our product. This creates more surface to have the same look for higher impact and compression strength.

Well-known architects like BBB architects, B+H, contractors like PCL and companies like Cadillac Fairview started using our products in 2015. The more people knew about the product, the more interest we received from different projects. We expanded into Quebec, the west coast of Canada, USA and Europe.

In 2010 I registered my company, Samia Canada, in Toronto as a potential oil and gas equipment trading company. I planned to focus on Samia Canada as my only business. A few years later, I settled down in Canada with $60,000 to live on and run my business. I rented a small shared office in North York and began doing research and marketing for it.

I needed money to invest in my idea. I travelled to South Korea and China to visit manufacturers. I had just moved to Canada with limited financial resources that I transferred from my country of birth. The value of what I started with decreased to one-third in less than 5 months due to the devaluation of my currency to Canadian dollars due to the sanctions against Iran and the economic crises going on at the time.

During one of my trips to China, at an expo in Shanghai, I met a man with a Persian background who made an enormous impact on my professional life. He was a businessman with fifteen years of experience in the Chinese market, especially in the import and export of cement and iron ore. In early 2013, he gave me an irresistible partnership offer. He said "Give me a 70% share in Samia Canada, and I'll invest $200,000 each year for three years. I'll help you with supplies from Asia, and you do the marketing in North America."

This was amazing. A dream come true. I was looking for investment to realize my ideas and introduce my product into the market.

But nothing went as expected. I rented a bigger office, after our agreement was on paper, and hired a team of marketing experts. Hoping to receive the investment. In February 2014, I planned to travel to China one last time to make the final business plan to this gentleman and his legal and financial team. I received a shocking phone call informing me that he was in the hospital, and the meeting needed to be postponed. At first, I thought "OK, this is not a big deal. We'll just do it a week later."

No news came in the following days. When I followed up, I discovered that he had been sent to jail for an undisclosed reason, without a release date. I had spent nearly $40,000 of my own money on the team and new office renovation, and I found myself feeling lonely and financially strained. I thought to myself, "You have two options, Sina. You can either declare bankruptcy, or close down the office, or, suck it up, and start from the scratch again."

I soon discovered that bankruptcy was not an option, since I only had 30% of the shares therefore, I was not qualified to declare bankruptcy. The only choice remaining was to make the difficult move and shut down the office.

I called my landlord the following day to cancel my lease, because I could no longer afford the rent. I also gave notice to my staff that I would close the company at the end of the month. With only $10,000 in the bank and an incarcerated business partner, I was in a very tough position.

The most common obstacle any businessperson has achieve their ideas and goals seems to be money and financial stability; however, in the middle of my crises, personal development courses helped me navigate the turbulence. I told myself "You can make this work." I was watching my sample piece of honeycomb for hours; I was taking it with me everywhere I went. I was telling myself, "It was you who made connections with all those international companies. You found the idea. You may have lost your partner and your financial resources, but you can still succeed with effort and belief."

Many times, in the early stages, I reached a point where I was asking myself if it was really worth it, the long hours working, not proportional rewards, non-payment by some clients, cash flow challenges and even physical back and neck pains. However, the passion and power I felt from inside and the level of independence I had was always inspiring me to continue and it paid off after 2.5 years.

I committed myself to study, learn and observe successful people and entrepreneur's lifestyles and also to working closely with mentors and coaches to keep motivation toward achieving my ideal lifestyle. Nothing was more valuable than a satisfied customer and a successful finished project. Any testimonial was a new light in my heart and kept the fire burning inside myself.

The path of entrepreneurship is all about action, failure, learning, experiencing, fixing and redoing. Many decisions and actions may take you toward your goals and many others will not. New products, fresh ideas, new services or innovative methods may not be accepted by the market; therefore, we have to keep our eyes open for changes. Over the years, I did the same, I tried partnerships, I trusted ideas that did not work, I learned from my failures. Having a commitment to progress is the critical point I want to make.

I remember I had a client who refused to pay for our job at the end of the project. It was approximately a $20k unpaid invoice, and I decided to take legal action. It cost us an extra $5000 for the lawyer and the paperwork. We won the trial but ended up receiving only $6000 and two blazers since the customer was a menswear boutique. The entire experience led to two very expensive casual coats, at $9000 per piece, plus a big lesson learned.

Over the years, we also tested different business models that we expected to work as they were working for some of our competitors. It is always good to look at the pioneers in your industry, but make sure you understand today's needs and requirements, trends, design tastes and also marketing tools and techniques. Look at what your audience has shown interest in from more recent days before you copy another businesses model. Being a follower without being smart will definitely result in failure, no matter how much effort you put in while moving in the wrong direction.

If I were to talk to my younger self, knowing what I know now, I would definitely encourage him to have a better and more effective mindset about sales, money and investment. For many years, I was concentrating on the quality of my services. My customers were always the centre of my attention, but I needed to focus more on compensation when I was younger, especially when I was making an extraordinary effort.

My belief system about salespeople and sales in general was a big preventive barrier for me to approach people. Ever since I really understood the value that I was offering to people and how important my product is in saving clients' money, time and human resources, I've been convinced that hesitating to request a sales conversation is avoiding providing a real benefit to them. The younger Sina could also work on his investing skills much earlier, but I have no complaint since access to knowledge 20 years ago was nothing like it is today!

I started to look closely at my habits and business systems in my mid-30s. However, it took a while until I educated myself about the triggers, routines and rewards for my bad habits and replaced them with the good ones. The most rewarding good habit for me was learning and accepting the fact that I needed to hire coaches and mentors to be able to develop myself and my life. I have a very unique habit and I love it. Whenever I face a major obstacle or a situation where many people may give up, instead of sitting back and getting involved in the problem itself, I give myself a maximum of 3 days to reach a solution and overcome the issue. Since I am set to solve my problems quickly, I have never given up at the end of the third day.

Time management for the entrepreneurs is essential. None of us have more than 24 hours a day and allocating our time and effort on less important tasks is a trap which will end up in procrastination and failing in transforming our dreams into reality.

Don't forget that we have two main assets in life, a body and a brain. Failing in protecting any one of these two brings us less chance of success. I am always looking carefully at the lifestyle of people that I have chosen as my role models and analyze the way they are living, behaving, thinking and maintaining their body and soul.

In my business, I have never entered into pricing games; the competition was always under observation though. It's essential to keep your eyes open wide and observe the needs and requirements of your clients, to feel them with your heart, and to try to create a solution for them. Years before people started talking about the role of "value" in business, I was trying to offer something beyond the customer's expectations. Something extra where they would feel comfortable talking to us as a partner, not a supplier or service provider.

We never promise something that we cannot deliver. That promise includes everything: the lead times, payment terms, product quality, packaging, installation time, etc.

Persistency and consistency are pillars for success in any business. Dwayne Johnson says, "Success is not about greatness, is about consistency. Consistent hard-work leads to success and greatness will come."

When communicating your message to your audience, it's always good to be precise and transparent. Transparency is an element of trust, and as soon as trust is built, business will thrive.

If these precepts worked for us and made us the #1 ranked company for honeycomb panels in Canada, it can work for the others too.

Learn More About Samia Canada, Inc. Products

Samia Canada, Inc. provides a range of honeycomb panels and other cladding solutions available on our website at: http://samiacanada.com/. If you are a contractor, builder, architect, or interior designer, a stone company, an elevator cab company or an industrialist that has an innovative idea for new surfacing solutions, or you're looking for strong and lightweight products, give us a call at (416) 548-5592 to discuss how we can best work together.

ABOUT THE AUTHOR

Sina Dejnabadi is an entrepreneur, industrial engineer as well as a certified import and export specialist in Canada. He is also certified by CITP and FIBP. Sina is an elite member of Forum for Canada's International Trade Training known as FITT. Sina is a qualified expert in interior design and decoration as well as an NLP and Time Line Therapy Practitioner.

Sina is the president and CEO of Samia Canada Inc., entitled as the "Number 1 one company" in supplying construction panels, known as honeycomb panels. He also owns an E-commerce, online retail, social media and digital marketing agency called Samicore. Moreover, Sina is the founder of a coaching platform named as First Class Seat Coaching in which he gives his audience consultancy on their personal and professional lives.

Sina's career life began back in 1996. As a very young man, who had decided to realise his dream, he started his quest and soon he saw himself gaining a wealth of experience in a variety of areas. In his journey, which has continued to date, Sina has made tremendous achievements in a wide range of fields including oil, gas, petrochemicals, quality assurance and ISO standards, construction, interior design, international business, as well as e-commerce and social media marketing. In a period of 23 years, Sina was significantly active in projects conducted by more than 20 European and multinational companies, including General Electrics (GE), Saint Gobain, Bosch Rexroth and so on and so forth.

Between the ages of 25 and 30, he took business trips to more than 18 countries in the world, where he garnered invaluable insights into various cultures and customs. Sina thinks of his experiences as "his greatest achievement".

Sina enjoys spending time with his family and his close friends. Travelling for pleasure and creating educational content are among what Sina does to pursue his hobbies.

Once asked if he could think of a single moment when he thought he was very lucky. He responded he is happy he had managed to flee from a spot one minute before it was bombed during Iran-Iraq 8-year-long war.

Sina's core philosophy of his personal and professional life is to leave memorable marks throughout his journey on the "fast train of life".

Should you wish to contact Sina and his team as well as his products and training courses, you can reach at:
www.samia-canada.com

(If you are in build or design business and looking for innovative construction and architectural products in residential and commercial projects)

LinkedIn: Sina Dejnabadi
YouTube: Sina Dejnabadi
Facebook: Sina Dejnabadi Official
Email: sina@samia-canada.com

Notes:

TAX MINIMIZATION FOR PROPERTY OWNERS
Anthony Gordon

Imagine walking up to a door, inserting the key into the lock, and gently turning the handle. You step into an empty house, and as you slowly move through each room, you begin to visualize where each of your favourite pieces of furniture will be placed as you start your new life. A dining table underneath that skylight, the side table by that bay window, the bed should face this direction, this will be the guest room, and that painting will look just right above the staircase. This is now your new home, the place you spent months searching for. You have looked at what felt like a thousand homes, placed millions of bids and felt you had found the perfect place, just before losing out to another bidder. After countless calls to and from realtors, a plethora of documents to initial, sign, and countersign, this is where you plan to create a future with your family. It may be the largest single purchase you have ever made, and will remain so until you purchase your next home.

The dream has come true, but it has cost you a significant chunk of your savings, or even all of your savings. Once the joy of having reached your goal of owning a home has faded (which may come sooner than you think!), you will be faced with the reality that you now have to build up your savings again. You will also have to consider other long-term goals like retirement, all while paying for a new mortgage, and handling additional costs that come with managing a home, which may include furniture, renovations and other unforeseen expenses. That painting looked just fine in the old place, come to think of it!

You are not alone in this predicament, as many Canadians share that concern of not having enough money for retirement. According to data compiled by the Advisor's Edge (Sunlife Barometer) in November 2019, 47% of working Canadians believe they are at risk of outliving their retirement savings, and 44% expect to be employed full-time at age 66, 65% of whom said it was not because they would enjoy being employed. If that wasn't sobering enough, 72% of Canadians who have retired say that their retirement is not what they were expecting.

While there are many factors that affect the value of your assets at retirement, ask yourself this question: what is the biggest expense? When I ask this question, the response I typically get is, "My mortgage!" Given that this book is about real estate, perhaps that was your response too. However, that is not so. Most of our income is spent on taxes. According to the Fraser Institute, just over 44 cents of every dollar that Canadians earn go to taxes. The taxes Canadians pay have increased by over 2200% between 1961 and 2018, while the cost of housing has increased by 1593%. So, how does this compare to the average cash income between 1961 and 2018? The average income during this period has increased by 1677%. Thus, it is not surprising that 47% of working Canadians believe that they are at risk of outliving their retirement savings, and that 72% of retired Canadians aren't living the retirement they envisaged. What may be surprising is the cause, as very few realize that taxes have outpaced income, leaving Canadians with less money in their pockets.

In this chapter, I want to provide Canadian homeowners with a few strategies that they can implement either before or after they have purchased a home, to help them lower their taxes and create additional cash flow that can be put towards retirement or a financial goal.

The first step in planning for your retirement should always involve deciding what it should look like. In "The 7 Habits of Highly Effective People," Stephen Covey advocated starting any process with the end in mind. In order to do that, what I recommend is a written financial game plan. This carefully considered game plan, which should be as detailed as possible, should serve as a financial GPS taking you from where you are now to where you want to go. It is never too early for a working adult to have a written plan. If you were driving from Toronto to New York, would you rather have the GPS when you start, or would you rather start using it after you end up in someone's backyard in Mount Pocono, Pennsylvania, in the middle of a snowstorm? I have a feeling that you would prefer the former. Either way, you are always better off with the GPS, no matter how late you start relying on it.

Now, part of that game plan should be a tax minimization strategy, especially given how much taxes Canadians pay. As paying less tax can considerably increase your income, it is not surprising that many tax minimization strategies are available. In this chapter, I will focus on only five for brevity: (1) Tax Deferral, (2) Income Splitting, (3) Income Spreading, (4) Tax Sheltering, and (5) Tax Credit Maximization. With each strategy, there is a myriad of ways to minimize your taxes. You will not be able to implement all the strategies, but if you were to implement 5–8, you will already see a dramatic improvement. In some instances, however, implementing just one strategy could mean thousands of extra dollars in your pocket.

Tax Deferral

The first strategy involves tax deferral, which allows you to avoid paying taxes on your income until some time in the future. By not paying taxes now, you are freeing some of today's hard-earned income for other investments, allowing it to compound and grow.

There are several ways to use tax deferral as a tax minimization strategy. One of the most common ones among homeowners is the Registered Retirement Savings Plan (RRSP). An RRSP, although the name denotes retirement, does not necessarily have to be used for that purpose; it can be used for many others, such as financing a home.

However, before we get into the use of RRSPs, let's begin with how you set them up, and how much you can contribute. An RRSP can be set up with a financial advisor, mutual fund distributor, life insurance agent, and almost any bank or trust company. You will have to fill out the forms necessary to open the account, to contribute a sum of money into the account, and to choose how to invest it. You will typically receive a copy of the documents you signed, and once you contribute, most institutions will provide you with a tax receipt.

The contributions you make to an RRSP are deductible for any given year if made that year or within 60 days after the year has ended. This contribution is limited by (1) a set dollar amount, (2) a percentage of the previous year's earned income, and (3) any type of pension adjustment. Let's start with the dollar limit, which is prescribed by the government annually: for 2020, that limit is $27,230, and it was $26,500 for 2019. The contribution is also limited by a percentage of the previous year's income; for 2019, that percentage is 18%. Once you have calculated the maximum contribution limit of 18% or the previous year's earned income, you must then subtract your pension adjustment for the previous year. This pension adjustment accounts for other retirement savings vehicles you may have contributed to, such as defined benefits plans and defined contributions plans, typically provided by your employer. Your pension adjustment will be indicated in your T4 slip.

If you have not contributed to your RRSP up to your contribution limit, that allowance can be carried forward, increasing your contributions for any following year.

Your contribution to an RRSP can result in tax savings depending on your marginal tax rates. Tax rates and tax brackets vary depending on your province and how much you earn annually. Generally, the amount you contribute to your RRSP directly reduces your net income. The lower your net income, the less income tax you have to pay. If you are an employee, your employer likely collects your taxes directly from your pay, and remits them to the government. However, after filing your tax return, the calculation may determine that your income was lower due to the RRSP tax deduction. As a result, the taxes you owe for the year are lower than what your employer collected, which leads to a tax refund representing the amount of taxes you overpaid for that year.

Now, if you withdraw money from your RRSP, the amount withdrawn will be included in your income for that year, and it will be taxed as ordinary income, just as if it were salary. And just like the pay from your employer, a percentage will be withheld by the financial institution and remitted to the government on your behalf. (Speak to your financial advisor or your accountant about the tax ramifications of withdrawing from an RRSP.) You must wind up an RRSP by the end of the year that you turn 71. Any time before then, you are allowed to transfer your RRSP, tax-free, to a registered retirement income fund, a life income fund, or an annuity.

While money withdrawn from an RRSP is typically treated as ordinary income, the government has allowed RRSP withdrawals up to a certain amount to be tax-free if those funds are used for certain purposes. One such purpose is the purchase of a home, and it is facilitated by the Home Buyers' Plan. For 2020, for withdrawals made after March 19, 2019, individuals who qualify can withdraw up to

$35,000 to buy or build a home, without the withdrawal being treated as income. You will then have 15 years to repay the funds, starting from the second year after the year you made the withdrawal. You may only use the Home Buyers' Plan if you are considered a first-time buyer, i.e., if you have not owned a home that was your principal place of residence at any time during the last five calendar years. Note, if you lived in a home owned by your spouse during that period, you will not qualify either. If you and your spouse each have RRSPs and will own the home together, you can each borrow up to $35,000. If you do not have the full $35,000 in your RRSPs and you intend to use the plan for 2020, then for the Home Buyers' Plan to apply, you must make your RRSP contributions at least 90 days before you withdraw the funds. You must also purchase the qualifying home before October 1st of the year following the year of the RRSP withdrawal, and you must begin or intend to occupy the home as a principal residence no later than one year after its acquisition.

RRSPs can also be used as a means of deferring income, thus allowing individuals to build their own pension plans. While money is in an RRSP, it can accrue interest without being subject to any tax, which can dramatically increase your savings over the years.

Another method of tax deferral is holding real estate, excluding your principal residence (which will be discussed later), which has the potential for long-term tax deferral of capital gains. For example, if you own a rental property that has increased in value twenty-fold from the time it was bought, at no point during that time do you have to pay taxes. Only when you sell the property are any gains taxable, and then likely only as a capital gain, calculated as the difference between the proceeds of disposition (normally the sale price) and the sum of the selling expenses and the adjusted cost basis (cost of the property plus any adjustments). Capital gains, in many cases, are taxed at a lower rate than regular income, and one-half of the capital gain is included in the taxable portion of an individual's income.

Tax Sheltering

The second tax minimization strategy is tax sheltering, whereby the government provides special tax benefits to taxpayers in certain circumstances, allowing them to pay little or no taxes. This would apply to the sale of a home, which is sheltered from any form of capital gain tax, provided that your home meets the definition of principal residence. The principal residence is, for tax purposes, the home where you spend most of your time and can be a house, a condominium, or a share in a cooperative housing corporation. This exemption also includes the land around the house, usually up to about 1.2 acres. Each family unit is permitted to have only one such principal residence. A family unit is defined as you, your spouse (including a common-law spouse) and any unmarried children under 18. Hence, if you designate your home as a principal residence, your spouse will not be allowed to claim another property as his/her principal residence. The tax saving opportunity here stems from the sale of your home with huge tax savings, allowing you to use portion of the released funds to assist with the retirement.

Another great tax sheltering strategy is the Tax-Free Savings Account (TFSA). This is a flexible vehicle that allows an individual to withdraw the income earned, at any time, tax-free. This may also be a great place to put the money received from a tax refund given by the government from an RRSP contribution. For example, if you took advantage of the Home Buyers' Plan, just after contributing to your RRSP, you may have been able to get a tax reduction, which led to a tax refund, which you can put aside as an emergency fund to help cover future costs associated with owning a home, or simply for your down-payment. All these options should be discussed with a financial professional, but the main takeaway here is that you have choices.

Income Splitting

Another strategy to consider is income splitting, where you shift income from one family member in a higher tax bracket to another family member who is in a lower tax bracket, as this will effectively reduce the tax paid on your income. The federal Income Tax Act has measures in place to make sure that this is not abused; specifically, there are attribution rules to consider if you are going to take advantage of income splitting. Despite these restrictions, there are still ways to benefit from this strategy.

A simple strategy to use here is the Primary Residence Equity Split. Regardless of the amount that each member of a couple paid for the principal residence, any equity retained after the sale of a home that met the principal residence exemption can be equally divided between the spouses, which will allow any future investments made by either spouse to be taxed accordingly. To fully benefit from this strategy, a spouse with a lower income (and thus lower marginal tax rate) should invest his/her earnings, which will then generate more income due to lower taxation.

Income Spreading

The third strategy is income spreading, as a part of which taxpayers are permitted to spread their income over several years, thereby preventing a spike in taxes payable for one year. This is particularly useful for homeowners who are self-employed, or business owners who will have years where they have unusually large payouts. This is a great way to ensure that, for that outlier year, you don't have to deal with an unusually large tax bill.

This strategy can also be used if you own capital property, such as a rental property, if (1) you are a resident of Canada at the end of the year or any time in the following year, (2) you were not exempt from paying tax at the end of the tax year, or at any time in the following year, and (3) you did not sell the capital property to a corporation that you control in any way. If you meet these criteria, when you sell the property for a capital gain, but do not receive all the proceeds of the sale immediately, you may be able to claim a reserve and defer recognizing the gain from the sale for tax purposes. Under the current rules, you must recognize at least $\frac{1}{5}$ of the capital gain each year, which will necessitate that all the capital gain be recognized by the fourth year after the sale. This strategy may not be in your best financial interest if you expect to be in a higher tax bracket in later years, or if it will cause a clawback for things like your Old Age Security benefits.

Tax Credit

The fifth and final strategy that homeowners should consider is tax credit maximization, which refers to any amounts that reduce the tax you pay on your taxable income. The greater the number of tax credits you are eligible for, the lower your taxable income.

An example of a tax credit that can be used by first-time home buyers is the First-Time Home Buyers' Credit. It is a non-refundable tax credit for first-time home buyers on up to $5000 of the home's cost (worth up to $750). Either the taxpayer or the spouse can claim it. To qualify, neither you nor your spouse are permitted to have lived in another home that your or your spouse owned in the preceding four years. A home qualifies if it meets the qualification of the Home Buyers' Plan discussed earlier. This credit can also be claimed for certain home purchases by or for the benefit of a disabled family member who is eligible for disability tax credit.

Conclusion

Owning a home can represent the achievement of a dream. A home can be a place that holds new memories for you and your family, the beginning of a new future. But from a purely financial perspective, owning a home is also a great way to deal with inflation and to help you achieve your financial goals. Using some of the strategies presented above will help reduce the stress you may face as a new homeowner, by minimizing your greatest expense (taxes!) and by freeing up funds that you can then use towards retirement or another goal, including (why not?) the purchase of another painting for that space above the staircase.

Notes:

ABOUT THE AUTHOR

A trusted financial advisor, and co-founder and CEO of FiduSure Financial.

Anthony believes in the desire of Canadian families to own their own home, educate their children, save for a comfortable retirement, and along the way, enjoy a meaningful and vibrant life. He believes that with the right plan, efforts and actions, it is both reasonable and realistic for each family to achieve their financial goals.

Heavy taxation, increasing debt, and cash-flow insecurity have created undue financial stress and uncertainty for families. Through tax minimization, investment planning, risk management and retirement planning processes, FiduSure co-creates the financial future with clients to ensure their dreams become reality. And throughout the journey, they help provide clarity and financial wellbeing.

Prior to establishing FiduSure, Anthony was a Financial Advisor for 6 years. He was also a lawyer with Canada's largest telecommunication company, providing legal and strategic advice to sales, product and procurement teams across the company, as well as negotiating and drafting a variety of agreements with strategic vendors and customers.

He holds a Bachelor of Business Administration from Bernard Baruch College, a Bachelor of Arts in Sociology from the

University of Buffalo, a Juris Doctorate from Thomas M. Cooley Law School, and a Masters of Law in Taxation from the University of Florida.

The breadth of his personal and professional experiences results in a unique ability to be attuned to the needs of his diverse clientele, and to serve them in a way that is highly personal.

When Anthony is not helping his financial advisors grow their business, he helps other lawyers, business owners, self-employed individuals and families achieve and maintain financial independence.

New Thinking. Unique Solutions. Exceptional Support.

Notes:

A HOMEOWNER'S GUIDE ON HOW TO CHOOSE A PAINTER AND AVOID GETTING TAKEN ADVANTAGE OF

Brian Young

The Purpose of Reading this Chapter

I have a severe passion for homeowners and changing their lives for the better. Currently I run a well-established residential painting company called *Home Painters* and we've had the good fortune of satisfying more than 15,000 clients over the past 30 years. I've also had the privilege of consulting with over 35,000 clients personally.

It's been a long journey. I've been able to personally witness the results of homeowners who have made some really good home improvement decisions, and unfortunately, some VERY bad ones as well. The purpose of this chapter is to prepare you to make the right decisions when it comes time to choose a painter, and to provide you with insight on what to do in planning your next home improvement project.

The skills that I will teach you here are also applicable to other trades. Whether you're hiring a painter, a plumber, or an electrician, the same basic rules apply.

At the end of this chapter, you as a homeowner will know how to choose a painter, what to look for, which questions to ask, and what clues to watch out for so that you can avoid making a decision that could put you in deep financial constraint and cause you a lot of unnecessary stress.

I will also talk about three inside secrets that painters don't want you to know. Knowing these tips will greatly stack the odds in your favour and ensure that you get the best painting contractor for the best value.

As a bonus, you will also learn seven tips on how to get a better price from your painter once you have chosen them for the job. These tips alone will be worth the time invested in reading the entire chapter in my opinion.

Why it is Imperative for You, as a Homeowner, to Get this Right

As I said before, I've been in this industry for 30 years, working with tens of thousands of homeowners like yourself who have made both good and bad decisions.

The reason why my message to you is so crucial is because I believe that your home is your biggest personal life possession. There are almost no other assets that are more valuable than your house and no other place you and your family spend the majority of your free time.

Another reason this chapter is vital is because with the evolution of the home improvement industry and the internet, there are more scammers and unscrupulous contractors right now than any other time in the history of residential painting. The fact is that anyone can call themselves a painter or open up a business online. This makes homeowners, like yourself, vulnerable to scam artists who don't back up what they say or purposely mislead clients.

Now let's get into the meat of the chapter so that you can learn how to educate yourself and become a street savvy and sharp homeowner.

Ten Questions to Ask Your Painter Before Hiring them

Let's face it: the contracting industry is not always honest and can sometimes a bit shady. There are no guarantees of anything in life, but if you follow my ten step question guide, then you have a far better chance at successfully hiring a painting contractor who will be able to take your home improvement needs to the next level.

Question #1: How long have you been in business?

- Make sure that the company has a master business license and ask to see it.

- There are big risks in the contracting industry, and unfortunately, that means there are no guarantees. One way to lower your risk is by going with well-established companies that have been around for long periods of time. There is no hard fast rule, but a reasonable level of time to be in business is about **ten years**. Any company that has been around less than ten years risks easily going out of business, which means that your warranty will be void.

- The other risks in choosing a company that's been around for less than ten years is that there is a lot less incentive to deliver the results they've promised: they may cut corners that they shouldn't, they may use cheaper products without your knowledge, and they may provide a lower quality workmanship and try to fool you since you're not an expert in the industry.

- How do you know how long a company has been in business?

    o Go online and see how far back their reviews go.
    o Ask them for their master business license or letter of incorporation and see the registration

date. Most companies that are established will easily have those certifications available for their clients to view.

Question #2: Do you have WSIB coverage?

- Did you know that if a contractor works on your property without workers compensation and someone gets injured, fakes an injury – or even worse – dies, then YOU are personally liable?

- It is necessary that a painting contractor provides you with their WSIB clearance before they step foot on your property.

- Painters are put in risky positions since they are often on ladders – in many cases two to three stories high. While accidents don't happen often, they *do* happen! The chances that someone gets injured or fakes being injured are low, but it simply isn't worth the risk to hire a painting contractor without WSIB coverage.

- Unfortunately, the reality is that more than 66% of general contractors do NOT have WSIB coverage, and when it comes to specifically painters, this percentage is much higher.

- If the company does not provide a WSIB clearance certificate, hire someone else for the job. The cost of being liable is just too high and not worth risking years of litigation.

Question #3: Do you have general liability insurance?

- It is crucial that a painting company has general liability insurance. The average paint job costs anywhere between $1,000 and $5,000. If anything were to happen – whether it be a paint spill, property damage, a paint can falling on someone's head, broken items, a fire, a flood, or any other potential issue that you can think of, then *you* are responsible for the related costs – unless the contractor has general liability insurance.

- The average property in The Greater Toronto Area values between $750 thousand and $2 million. Protecting your most valuable asset and what is inside it from damage and liability just makes sense. Despite this fact, more than 80% of painting contractors don't have liability insurance in Ontario.

- Keep in mind, the chances of mishaps happening are quite low, but if they do occur, then the only leverage you have as a homeowner to recoup that expense is the cost of the paint job. In most cases, this cost is far less than the value of the house and its belongings. If your contractor has liability insurance, then you and your home are protected financially.

- The minimum liability insurance a painting contractor they should have is $2 million in coverage. Considering the costs values of homes currently, however, $5 million coverage is more advisable. Any reputable painting contractor will have at least $5 million liability insurance.

- The bottom line, make sure that your contractor shows you the up-to-date proof of insurance certificate. Like car insurance, general liability insurance needs to be renewed each year. If their insurance is expired, then you are just as vulnerable as you would be if they never had it in the first place.

Question #4: Do you perform criminal background checks on your staff?

- With the emergence of both online and offline scams, thieves, and unscrupulous workers nowadays, the need for criminal background checks are becoming more and more important. Would you trust a stranger in your home? Maybe. But what if they were unsupervised? Probably not! Background checks are important in determining whether the company is reputable and good at what they do.

- Did you know one out of every ten tradespersons do have a criminal record? This means that the chances that you could come across one is fairly high.

- Make sure that your painting contractor performs criminal background checks on their workers. This gives you peace of mind and increases the odds that you have trustworthy people working inside your home.

Question #5: Can I see your reviews?

- With the power of the internet and online marketing, pretty much any painter you hire will have good and bad reviews.

- Think about it, if you got scammed or misrepresented when dealing with a company, what would you do? Probably write a negative review to warn others and stop the company from continuing on with their bad behaviour.

- The truth is, most people don't write good reviews unless they are really happy and want to give something back. On the other hand, if they are unhappy or feel like they got ripped-off, then they will almost always leave a bad review.

- It's important that you check both the good ones AND the bad ones. Keep in mind that if you are hard-pressed for time, then it's much more important to *check their bad reviews first.* Why? Because these bad reviews are most likely the worse-case scenarios that a company has had to deal with.

- Do great companies make mistakes or sometimes have unreasonable clients? Of course! But this is why to check their bad reviews. When checking, see if the company responds in a positive way and are not being overly-defensive or vindictive. This will tell you whether this is the type of company that you want to deal with not. You want to hire someone who stands behind their work, is reasonable, and tries to resolve their conflicts amicably.

Question #6: Do you have any warranties and guarantees?

- Every painter should have a solid warranty of at least two years on interior and exterior services. There are exceptions, like guarantees against rust, and high-traffic areas where wear-and-tear is inevitable. But, for the most part, the warranty shouldn't be too restrictive and limiting. After all, there are always ways for companies to get out of a warranty claim if this is the case.

- The other thing is to make sure that they have been around for at least 10 years. Remember: the warranty is only as good as the company. With 95% of small businesses failing within the first 5 years, it's important to make sure they have been around for a long time and will be around for the foreseeable future.

- Companies who don't back up their work typically get a lot of backlash from their client reviews. Alternatively, if clients praise them for their ability to follow-through with their warranties and promises, then you know that company is a reputable one and that you will be safe should there be any issues down the road.

Question #7: Have you worked or partnered with any known, reputable brands?

- One sign of a solid company is that they've worked with other established and trusted brands. This may include any HGTV shows, TV or radio stations, or retailers such as The Home Depot or Lowes. After all, would a well-known and trusted brand risk their reputation by working with an unscrupulous painter or tradesperson? Of course not!

Question #8: Do you provide written contracts?

- The contract is fundamental when working with any trade. Some contractors will give you a verbal quote, or just as bad, hand write a number on the back of a business card. This is the easiest way to get scammed, misled, or ripped-off because you are not provided with a contract with clear guidelines and expectations.

- Even if you are provided with a contract, be sure to read the fine print. If there are too many conditions, see if you can get them to waive some of them. Sadly, many contracts are easy for the contractor to get out of should there be a warranty claim. For example, in the painting business, phrases such as "no warranty on window ledges and previous moisture negates warranty" allows the contractor to get out of the warranty claim with ease.

Question #9: Are you involved in the community or any social causes?

- Most reliable painters will be involved in the community and charitable events that involve giving back. This shows they are genuinely good businesses made up of good people who value providing good service and like to help out their community as a result of their success.

- Any dishonest painting contractors will do the opposite of giving back. They will hide, cheat, steal, and avoid public interaction and involvement because they have a bad reputation.

Question #10: What are your payment terms - cash, cheque, credit card?

- Payment terms aren't everything, but the fact that a painting company can offer you multiple payment options makes it less likely that you're dealing with a bad painting contractor.

- The fact that a contractor can offer credit card payments alone means that they are not struggling financially as a business and have a decent credit history.

Want some added value? Check out this animated video for "five tips on how to choose a painter."

https://homepainterstoronto.wistia.com/medias/z5uv6g1x9q

Three Inside Secrets that Your Painting Contractor does NOT want You to Know

1. Find Out How Far Ahead They are Booking

   - Ask your painter when they think they could start your project. If it's within a week or two, then you have a lot more bargaining power than if they were booked a month or greater in advance.

   - Why doesn't your painter want you to know how far ahead they're booked? If they aren't securing many jobs, they may be forced to price jobs tighter and take on projects for a lower cost than usual simply because they need the money. For example, let's say a painter is only booked until Friday, and it is Tuesday or Wednesday already. If you know this, then you may be able to negotiate a lower, more competitive price with them because they know that they need to book the job with you in order to keep their business running. If the contractor is booked for the rest of the month, however, they can risk saying "no" because they know they have a steady income coming in regardless.

2. Know Who Their Top Competitors are

   - If you are getting three quotes, I recommend hinting to the painter that you are considering their competitors as well. Like any business, painting is a very competitive industry. Many painters will sometimes price a job a little lower than usual if they know one of their top competitors are also bidding on the job.

   - In many cases, painting contractors will also give you more consideration over other jobs just to win your project from their competitors.

   - Knowing the competition is a sneaky way of getting everything you want out of your painting contractor, but is completely reasonable and ethical in my opinion.

3. November to March is a Slower Time of Year for Painters

   - If you book your quote and job during the period between November and March, there is a strong likelihood that you will have a much better bargaining position.

   - For the most part, painting is a seasonal business. The months from April to October are by far the busiest months for a painter.

- Most painting businesses need to lay off a large portion of their staff during the slow winter months when they're not pulling in as many jobs. As a result, this is the best time for you to hire a painter. You could be looking at a HUGE discount on your pricing – sometimes as much as 30-40%.

- I'll be honest: although my company does have standard pricing, I've sometimes lowered my price far below what I normally charge just to keep my staff working during the slow months of the painting season.

Seven Tips on Getting a Cheaper Price from Your Painter

Now that you have done your homework, chosen your painter and feel confident that they are going to do a stellar job for you. Now what? Here are seven tips on getting a better price from them just before you sign that contract.

Tip #1: Be flexible with your time.

- If you give time flexibility to your painter or contractor, there is a good chance that they will give you a bit of price break in return. This means that you could receive a cheaper home painting quote.

Tip #2: Clear out your rooms.

- One of the biggest time-wasters for painters is moving the furniture and preparing the rooms prior to painting the property. If your house is completely empty, however, you'll be more likely to get a cheaper quoting price. In an ideal situation, you can have the painter complete the project before you move in.

- If you already live in your home and you are looking to update, offer to move all or most of the furniture before they get there. This will save the contractor a lot of time and money, so they may be willing to lower the quote for you!

Tip #3: Let the painter choose the brand of paint.

- Some painting contractors get great discounts from different paint manufacturers. This doesn't mean that you will get a "cheap looking" paint job; it just means that one supplier may have worked out a better volume discount for your contractor than another. Next time you're getting a quote, ask your painter what brand they prefer.

Tip #4: Make your payment terms flexible.

- Most reputable painters will offer you a variety payment terms: Visa, MasterCard, Amex, or even postdated cheques.

- Paying by credit card means that the contractor has to pay extra processing fees, but if you pay by cheque, there are no "extra" costs for them. Don't be scared to ask your contractor if paying by cheques will affect the house painting price.

Tip #5: Get Multiple Painting Quotes.

- Get quotes from a few different companies to see what options are available within your budget. Or, at the very least, tell the contractor that you have your heart set on that you will have to get quotes from other companies unless they can lower their cost estimate a bit.

- If you can't be bothered getting other painting quotes and feel comfortable with your painter, you can simply ask whether they'd give you a discount if you sign with them now and forego reaching out to other companies for painting estimates. In some cases, you may just get what you ask for!

Tip #6: Painting MORE is better.

- To paint one more wall or one more room once all of the equipment is set up is quite minimal in the grand scheme of things. To get the best value, try adding on a few more painting projects than chopping off some that you think can wait until later. In general, painting more areas can cost just marginally a bit more. If you spread your painting projects out over the course of a year or two, however, you will be paying the contractor for the price to set up multiple times.

Tip #7: When all else fails, politely beg!

- You may think I'm kidding, but I'm serious about this one. If you politely say "*If you can give me a cheaper quote, I'll be happy to give you my business today,*" your contractor may just oblige you! Again, the key here is to be polite, while also explaining that you need a better deal than what they've already asked you. As simple as this sounds, many times you will get what you ask for.

Check out this cool animated video on these seven tips in action!
https://homepainterstoronto.wistia.com/medias/5vnwqlpj4d

Why You Should Consider Using *Home Painters*?

As mentioned in the introduction, I have an absolute passion for helping homeowners. It has been my lifelong mission to make their dreams come true.

And, that's why it's our mission at *Home Painters* to "paint homeowners' dreams!" My hope is that writing this chapter furthers that cause.

Here are some reasons why *Home Painters* has been rated the #1 painting contractor in the Greater Toronto Area and Southern Ontario for over three decades and what makes us unique from our competitors:

1. Our Speed

    -   We are open seven days a week to better serve you.

    -   We offer same-day quoting.

    -   We also offer one and two-day painting services.

    -   Simply put, from start to finish, we complete your project faster than any other company in the industry, bar none.

2. Our Quality and Warranties

    -   As skilled craft-persons with decades of experience, we are absolutely obsessed with quality. We are so confident that we will deliver you the top job that your house deserves, we offer an unprecedented **life-time warranty on our interior work.**

    -   Additionally, we offer a two-year and extended warranty on our exterior work.

3. Our Security

    -   We have been in the painting business for over 30 years, making us one of the longest-standing painting contractors in the Greater Toronto Area and all of Southern Ontario.

    -   We provide full workers' compensation (WSIB), $5 million general liability insurance, perform criminal background checks and ministry compliance checks to ensure the safety of you and our team on the worksite.

4. Our One-Stop Shop Service

- We are a full service, one-stop shop painting company that offers the widest range of services in our industry.

- We employ full-time carpenters and handymen, so that when you need drywall, plastering, crown moulding, wainscoting, or trim casings installed, we will be there to save you the hassle of dealing with multiple tradesmen and companies.

- We also specialize in niche services, such as brick staining, popcorn ceiling flattening, professional kitchen cabinet spraying, staircase and oak door re-furbishing and staining, and much, much more!

5. Our Flexibility of Payment

- We accept major credit cards and offer "no fee" credit card options.

- We offer no-interest payment plans up to one full year.

6. Our Unbeatable Customer Service and Reputation

- We have been named *HomeStars'* Best in Class three years in a row (2017, 2018, 2019, and 2020). This award recognizes our world-class customer service! Check out over 1,000 raving reviews from our clients on their website!

- We have worked with some of the top names in the industry including *Holmes on Homes*, *Breakfast Television*, *Custom Built* on *HGTV* with Paul Lafrance, The Marilyn Denis Show, *House and Home Magazine*, and more!

7. Our 100% Satisfaction Guarantee

   - We aren't satisfied until you are satisfied!

   - Our job isn't complete until you have done a thorough walk-through with us to make sure that you are 100% happy with all the work done by our team.

Still need more info? Check out this video on the 5 things that make *Home Painters* unique!

Video on 5 top uniques of HP

For a free no obligation quote, please contact us at <u>Sales@HomePaintersToronto.com,</u> or call us directly at 416-494-9095, and we will be happy to take care of you!

Conclusion

I really hope that this chapter has opened your eyes, educated you, and given you some insider tips on how to pick the right contractor to paint your house. As you can see, there are a lot of unknowns involved, which makes it all the more important that you take the necessary measures to find the best painting company.

I also hope to meet you one day! Maybe it will be this chapter that leads you to me. If we do happen to meet, please feel free to use these tips and tricks on me. I'd love to be challenged on my own advice!

Regardless, it was a pleasure to share some of the top tips I've learned over the years while working in this industry. Hopefully, they'll help steer you towards the right painting companies that you can count on to make your dream house a reality!

ABOUT THE AUTHOR

Brian Young is the CEO and Founder of <u>Home Painters</u>: a leading painting contractor in the Greater Toronto Area since 1991.

Brian started his career as a Student Painter back in 1987 while attending York University. Although, business started with lots of inspiration, like anything Home Painters had its share of ups and downs.

In September of 2011, Brian finally hit rock-bottom after receiving the ultimate wakeup call – being literally punched in the face by an irate prospective client for "cold-calling" his house. This was the wakeup call that Brian needed to start to innovate his business.

In January 2012, Brian hired a business coach, created a website, assembled an SEO team, and invested in a CRM software. Very quickly, his business began to soar. Within seven years, his revenues skyrocketed by over 800% while his work week was cut down by 40%.

Brian is now in high-demand for his views on entrepreneurship and business. He's been recently featured in many publications and on many websites, including Entrepreneur.com, The Globe and Mail, allBusiness.com, Small Biz Trends, Canadian Business Magazine, Business.com, Maclean's Magazine, and various interviews and podcasts.

Brian's story is inspirational and exemplifies what determination, constant innovation, and always helping his clients can do for your business.

Notes:

WHY YOU MUST HAVE INSURANCE
Edith Kernerman

Caveat Emptor: Mortgage Insurance is Anything but Insurance!

Congratulations! You bought a home. Whether it's a condo, or a semi-detached house, or a full detached, or a row house, or townhouse, whatever you bought you are about to call it home. Maybe you are upsizing or downsizing. Or perhaps you are buying this property to flip, or resell one day, or to create an income property. Unless you paid for the whole thing in cash you likely took out a loan, otherwise known as a mortgage. Welcome to getting into, or staying in the market, and welcome to the shadowy world of mortgage insurance, where *buyer beware* is the rule to follow.

What is Mortgage Insurance?

Mortgage insurance is a product which is supposedly put in place to pay off the balance of the mortgage in the event the person responsible for paying the mortgage dies. Some mortgage insurance companies also advertise they will pay a benefit to the payor if s/he becomes sick or injured and cannot pay their mortgage payments.

Mortgage insurance is almost always applied for alongside the mortgage. However, too often, clients won't realize they are buying mortgage insurance when they sign the documents. Furthermore, clients don't often know how mortgage insurance works or even if it is a suitable product for them to have.

The challenges around mortgage insurance are numerous, not the least of which is the person selling you the product is not a licensed insurance agent. It follows then that if any medical questions are asked on the document, a client is immediately at a disadvantage by not having someone licensed explain what the questions mean.

Frequently there will be only one medical question will appear as a long strand of phrases that bundles many medical conditions into one long run-on sentence. As well, this long sentence might inquire about seeing a medical professional in the previous 24 (or 36, or 48, etc.) months for any of those named conditions. The very nature of asking a question in this rather ambiguous way leads to confusion.

For instance, when Peter saw his physician 3 months before applying for his mortgage he had no idea that his visit would constitute an investigation into various types of cardiovascular conditions. Yet, two years later, when Peter's spouse filed a claim on the mortgage insurance after Peter died of a stroke, his spouse's claim was denied, stating Peter lied on the application. According to the insurance company, because a blood pressure cuff was used to check Peter's bloodwork that meant he was being investigated for high blood pressure and stroke—even though the visit to the doctor had been a routine check-up and none of his medications had been changed.

What makes matters even more complex is that every application is different and every time you apply for a mortgage, the bank representative or mortgage agent is obligated to offer you mortgage insurance; however, you are not obligated to accept it. In fact, my advice is to decline! But before you say yes or no to anything, it is important to understand why, and what else should be in place before you say 'no'.

You see, mortgage insurance was created as a product to protect the lender and the debt, not your family or anyone else who might be responsible for paying the mortgage. That bank representative/ mortgage agent, gets paid for this and they will make a few hundred dollars' commission when you sign that paper. Most often the institution where the mortgage agent works will have quotas and expectations for how many of these policies should be sold. The revenue from the sale of mortgage insurance is enormous. And most often this is because, as I stated earlier, most people will just sign on the dotted line without quite knowing what they are signing.

But what if you refuse to sign? Now the agent must reprint the insurance document and have you sign a page stating that you decline mortgage protection. Occasionally, some mortgage documents just have a box to tick so that a separate decline sheet doesn't have to be printed. Well, what if you do intend to refuse the insurance?

The mortgage agent might tell you:

> "You need protection. What if you die? What if you have a heart attack or stroke? Or you get cancer? Don't you want your family to be okay? Do you want him/her/them to bear the burden of the mortgage? I think you should take it, don't you?"

And the agent is right! Their concern is valid, but is this the best way to get protection?

The agent might also say:

> "Look, take it for now, and then go and get some *real* life insurance."

And that may not be such a bad thing. Take it now, get the agent paid (no skin off your back), and then quickly go and get something that will truly cover you.

Or, the agent might say:

"That's okay, I don't really care if you take this or not, but you should probably get some insurance to cover this mortgage."

This too, is valid. If you don't already have insurance in place, run—don't walk—to your most trusted advisor (no, not the bank), and get some term life insurance (more on that later) for the same amount as the mortgage and for the duration of the mortgage (and more on this later, too— because a good agent/advisor will have some strategies to pay less and get more).

Saying 'no' to this is sometimes more difficult than you might imagine. After all, you are not the expert here. You have sought out this mortgage agent because they were able to get you the money to buy your home or investment. And if they are recommending you take the insurance who are you to question? It can feel awkward to say 'no'. You may even start to second guess yourself—and so you sign. So, what's so bad about that? After all, a few lines up on this page I just stated that maybe that's not such a bad idea at all. Well, it isn't, unless you take it and then you forget to replace it. Or you put it off. Or a few weeks later you get sick or injured and suddenly, you no longer qualify for a real policy. And then it's too late. And the mortgage insurance becomes a nail-biting experience while you hope nothing goes wrong, instead of a blanket of comfort providing peace of mind that your family is protected in the event the worst happens.

What are the pitfalls of Mortgage Insurance?

Pitfall Number 1. Don't Blink! $150 Can Buy $500,000 Then Only $1000!

Your mortgage insurance premiums won't change as you pay down your mortgage. Let's say, for example, that your mortgage premium is $150 for a $500,000 mortgage. Even though you've done an excellent job getting that mortgage balance down from $500,000, to $300,000, to $100,000, and then below six figures, and so on, your premiums for the mortgage insurance are still exactly the same as when you first agreed to have that product. You will still be paying $150. Even if your mortgage balance is only $5000, your premiums will still be $150. What's crazy about this is if you die, and the lender decides to pay the death benefit, the balance remaining on the mortgage is the maximum that will be paid. In this case, $5000. Even though you are still paying the premium for the $500,000.

Pitfall Number 2. Show Me the Money!!

Who gets the money if you die? Your loved ones? Your partner/spouse? Your kids?

Guess again. It's the lender. Yes, that's the bank or mortgage company who gave you the mortgage. You see, the second reason why mortgage insurance is not a good product is that the beneficiary is not of your choosing. And what's wrong with that? The lender paid for the balance of your home so you could buy it. The lender should get paid, right? Well, not so right. What if you didn't want to pay the lender? What if your beneficiary had other plans and intended to keep the mortgage and use the money for other necessities. Shouldn't your beneficiary decide how they want to use the money?

I'm not suggesting that your death is a reason the lender shouldn't be paid at all. On the contrary, I'm questioning whether or not they need to be paid in full just because you died? What if your beneficiary would rather pay only part of the mortgage now? Maybe half, or a third. Or just keep the mortgage payments going as before because they could make better use of those funds in another way? Well, there is no option here. If the mortgage insurance pays out, the full amount is going to the lender. That's it. Final.

Are you wondering why on earth someone wouldn't want to pay off that huge mortgage balance and be rid of the debt once and for all? Sometimes there are situations where the money could be used for other things at that time. Putting the money away to earn interest as a source of income in the future might make a whole lot more sense. Let me tell you about Shelley and Bart. I think their story illustrates beautifully why you might not necessarily want to have a mortgage paid off and why it is so important to have the choice.

I was introduced to this beautiful couple a few years back. Shelley was the sweetest woman who worked very hard and adored Bart. Shelley's income took care of the household and the rent. Bart, who held Shelley up on a pedestal, was an artist who did a tremendous amount of charitable work and was never paid for his efforts. This was something the couple had decided was important to them and was their way to share their fortunate lives with the community. They were not of any real means—but they made enough to get by. And they were wonderfully happy. When I first met them they asked me to arrange some life insurance for them. We did a needs analysis and a financial game plan, and we planned for a house purchase in the somewhat-near future. At the time, we decided it would be best if they purchased an affordable term policy to cover a small amount of debt and to replace their income if one of them should die.

One day, Shelley called me and said they had bought a house—I was thrilled for them. Bart had taken on part-time paid work to help buy the home more quickly. They had worked so hard and their new home was to be their dream home. The plan was for Bart to take some time to do the renovations himself in between his job and his charity work, and that way there would be very little needed to pay for any renovations. Shelley told me they would have a sizeable mortgage and they would need to increase their life insurance because she had told the mortgage agent that they didn't want the mortgage insurance; I was so pleased they had taken my counsel from two years earlier and had remembered to refuse the mortgage insurance.

A few months later, after they had been in their new home for only a month Bart arrived home to find Shelley suddenly and horribly ill. She had never been sick a day in her life. Truly. And five weeks later I sat with Bart while he planned her funeral. Just like that Shelley was gone. Aside from the emotional devastation, Bart now had to figure out how to pay for a mortgage on his small income. Remember, his charity work was something the couple had decided was of paramount importance. Shelley hadn't planned to die; she had thought she was in excellent health and she had always felt great up until that time. She would bring in the income and he would build their contribution to the world.

I reminded Bart that he had a death benefit coming to him to cover the mortgage. He was relieved to know the mortgage debt would be gone, because he didn't see how he would be able to handle it on his own. As we began to work out a budget, Bart realised there were so many other monthly payments that Shelley had always covered and that Bart wouldn't be able to pay. He knew he needed to get a second job, or one that paid better than what he had. The charity work would have to be put on hold for at least a few years until he could get back on his feet. Maybe he would never be able to go back to it. Or maybe he would have to sell the house.

But I had another idea. If we set aside a small percentage of the funds to act as an emergency fund, put about a quarter of the money into a high interest savings account to supplement his income as needed during the next 2 years, then invest the rest over the long term. Bart would be able to start drawing a regular income from the investment 2 years later. The income would be enough to cover all his mortgage, property tax, utility bills, and basic living expenses. This plan would continue until the mortgage was paid off. And if he followed the plan to the letter, he would have almost the exact same amount of money left in his investments that we put in from the death benefit.

Bart would not have to face any financial hardship whatsoever. Even though the loss of Shelley had been emotional devastating, the loss of her income would not be financially devastating.

This strategy would not have been possible if Shelley and Bart had taken out traditional mortgage insurance. Bart would almost certainly have been forced to sell the dream home they had worked so hard to buy.

Even worse, and incredible to believe, the mortgage insurance almost definitely would not have paid the claim.

Pitfall Number 3. Maybe We Will and Maybe We Won't

It's true. The mortgage insurance company will not necessarily pay the claim. There's no guarantee it will pay the balance of the mortgage, or even part of it. It might and it might not. What do I mean by that? The most diligent client can pay their premiums on time every month without fail and when it comes time to make a claim, their beneficiary might receive a letter stating: "Your recent application for mortgage # 1234567 in the amount of $376,420 has been denied." Or something like that.

Even though you paid your premiums the insurance company doesn't check to see if you actually qualify for their mortgage insurance. They will only verify that qualification after you die or become sick, not before. This is a practice called Post-Claim Underwriting. And in my opinion, it is one of the worse products on the market and it borders on unethical.

With all other life insurance, the medical underwriting is done by the insurance carrier, or by a licensed agent, on behalf of the insurance carrier, who can help you determine if you qualify for the product you plan to purchase. Then the insurance company conducts whatever degree of underwriting they require to enter into a contractual arrangement with you where they guarantee your claim will be paid regardless of how you died. They might request blood work, a paramed appointment, even a letter from your doctor. Then they will offer you a policy with coverage and premiums that are reflective of your health and needs. It's a contract that clearly states the Insurance carrier will pay the claim in the event of your death, as long as the policy is in force, and the policy will stay in force as long as you pay your premiums. Simple.

On the other hand, mortgage insurance will look at your health history after you die.   The underwriters might determine that the routine blood-work during your check-up by your doctor a year before you took out the policy was an investigation for high cholesterol and should have been disclosed on the application. Claim denied.

Sometimes they will be generous and pay 25%, or 50% or 0. Worse, the company is not even required to report to any regulatory body how often they do or do not pay these claims.

If it wasn't such a serious matter I would say it was a joke.

A colleague of mine had a bizarre case where her client called her in hysterics. Not only had her husband suddenly died at his workplace while at his factory job, but now the bank who gave her the mortgage refused to pay the balance owing. Margaret and Dan had agreed to have mortgage insurance when they renegotiated their mortgaged five years earlier. Four years later, Dan lost his footing on a step ladder at work when a bunch of barrels way above him fell down and crushed him. He died immediately. It was such a horrific accident. He had been in tremendous physical condition, was an avid runner and athlete, and very agile but couldn't get out of the way in time. Well, the insurance company saw it differently. They denied Margaret's claim outright. What was their rationale? They claimed that Dan must have experienced some dizzy spells due to low blood pressure and that the barrels must have fallen as a result of Dan falling off the ladder. They determined that he must have had a pre-existing condition before he and Margaret applied for the mortgage insurance and their lender, one of Canada's largest banks, refused to pay the claim.

Luckily, my astute colleague insisted the family take the bank to court and Margaret ended up winning the claim. That was great news for Margaret. However, the banks and other lenders rely on the fact that most people will not go to court—either they feel they won't win, or they don't have the money for a lengthy trial, or they are too exhausted or emotionally distraught to even consider doing so. No wonder the banks strongly encourage their employees to sell mortgage insurance to every one of their mortgage customers. They are banking on you not fighting to hold them accountable.

What are the Alternatives?

By now, I hope you will agree, there is little to no reason to ever consider agreeing to purchase such a product. But you might ask, shouldn't I have something?

The answer is an emphatic 'Yes!'

Let's take a little step back and do a quick synopsis of what true mortgage protection, i.e. life insurance, is and what it could and should be. Life insurance is a product that pays a death benefit upon the death of the person who is insured. Often it is used to replace the insured person's income if they die because it is the lack of that income that has the most financially devastating effect on the deceased's family. It's not as though your employer is going to be knocking on your door every two weeks after you die to hand your spouse and kids a cheque. Sorry to say, that is never going to happen. We therefore put coverage in place to replace that income if we die.

To make an application for such coverage, a licensed insurance agent will ask you questions about your finances so that s/he can help determine with you how much coverage you will need: what is the balance on your mortgage; what is your annual income; the value of your assets, like your home and other investments; your debt; how many dependents you have and who are they. The insurance agent is not being nosey, they're doing the job they're required by law to do.

Insurance can be purchased for a temporary need, like covering the debt on a 20-year mortgage, or putting kids through post-secondary education. These are temporary situations that can be covered with a term life policy. Term life insurance is a relatively inexpensive way to make sure that no one else will have to pay for these debts if you die. There are other debts we might have that might require a permanent policy. Funeral expenses are the most logical need for a permanent policy because you probably don't know the day you will die and because you likely don't want anyone else to have to pay for your funeral. As well, certain taxable events may be other reasons to have a permanent policy. Because many of your investments will have deemed dispositions at death—meaning they will be considered "cashed in" or redeemed if you don't have a spouse who can assume them—there will be a taxable burden on your estate. That means less money for your beneficiaries. As well, payments might be needed to cover the executor of your estate, the sale of your home and its contents, capital gains on investment properties, RRSPs that won't roll over because there is no surviving spouse— these can create a large tax burden on your estate, and in the end, less money to your heirs. A permanent policy can pay for such an expense and ease that burden.

Living Benefits

Guess what the number one reason why peoples' homes go into foreclosure. No, it's not because people lose their jobs. It's because people become too sick or injured to work. What needs protection is a person's ability to pay for their expenses and family's needs. The focus should not be solely on life insurance (which is really death insurance, if you think about it) but instead on what will happen if you become sick or injured and *you don't die*! Because although on average 1 in 9 Canadians will die before the age of 65, 1 in 3 people will become disabled for 90 days or longer before the age of 65!

Moreover, between 1 in 3 and 1 in 4 will become critically ill before the age of 64.

Injury can happen to us at any age—it doesn't care. Jake is very dear friend of mine. He is a wonderful professional dancer, and a yoga and fitness instructor. He is in spectacular shape and as healthy as anyone I know. He works out at the gym daily, is a vegetarian who cares what he puts in his body, he meditates daily, has a beautifully happy disposition, and his mindset keeps him exuding positivity from his core. How shocked was I to learn that when he had been riding his bike last summer out of the blue he swerved to avoid a car door, hit a ditch sending his amazingly fit body through the air landing on his side and broke his hip. This was even more extraordinary because there's no osteoporosis in his family. Consequently, he had to be off his feet for weeks after his surgery, then on crutches for the next three months and a cane another couple after that. Imagine being in that situation and having a mortgage but not being able to bring in your income at all. No work for him. And no alternative pay either. Why? He didn't have disability coverage. Based on his income, a disability policy would have paid him $3500/month for as long as he couldn't work at his own occupation. And it would have covered him from day one onward due to this injury being an accident that required an overnight stay in the hospital. It also would have paid him up until the age of 65 if necessary.

This brings me to why we need to have full mortgage protection. What is full mortgage protection, you may ask? What does it encompass?

- Properly underwritten life insurance that is guaranteed to pay upon death;

- Disability insurance that covers illness and accident and Injury; and

- Critical illness coverage that will pay a lump sum in the event of a serious event like a heart attack, cancer, or stroke.

I want to talk for just a little bit here about critical illness. I used to feel that critical illness was like the Cadillac of insurance and only for people who could truly afford to pay for it properly. In other words, if a person had maxed out all their other registered plans, they had excesses of money in their Investments, and all the disability and life insurance that they needed, then, and only then, did it seem to me that it would make sense to carry critical illness insurance.

I was wrong. I have come full circle. Seeing the statistics in Canada on how many people come to have a critical illness, even temporarily, is astounding. Whether that is due to heart disease, stroke, metastatic cancer, schizophrenia, or multiple sclerosis, too many will suffer financial hardship while taking time off work to go to the doctor, or specialists, or get treatment. Just think, six weeks after a heart attack you might be able to go back to work. But what about some of the follow-up visits to a specialist? Or perhaps you have a stroke that takes a few months to start getting mobility back in your arm or leg, or vision back in your eye. You might not be able to drive your car for some time—or ever again. How will you pay for a driver to take you to work or your appointments? A disability policy will not cover the payments to a driver, or put more money in your bank account so you can take Uber every day. But a well-designed critical illness policy that will give you a lump-sum payment of $25,000 or $50,000, or even $100,000 or $200,000 will help mitigate these costs while you ease yourself back to work. It's an excellent way to make sure that there is some income to supplement whatever work you can do. Your job is not likely to pay you to take time off every single week. After a while it will need to come from your own pocket. Or if you own your own business, you might need to hire someone in your place on a daily or weekly basis for several months or years as you adjust to your illness or disability.

For these reasons, I now recommend that my clients consider purchasing critical illness insurance even if it's a small policy of only $25,000 that only lasts for 10 or 15 years.

Something to consider: life insurance is for the people we leave behind. There is nothing wrong with that. In fact, I think it quite noble and the adult thing to do. However, living benefits like critical illness and disability are for us and for our immediate family while we are alive because we need to have income coming in if we can no longer work. It is also important to note that unlike your income from work, insurance benefits are non-taxable. This means that whether they are coming to you as an individual or coming to your beneficiaries these are not claimed as income. The logic of this argument is sound here and something where I wish we all could take heed.

Where Do You Go from Here?

First, find a top-notch insurance broker. One who is not tied to any one company, but instead can quote you on products from dozens of insurance carriers across the country.

Second, discuss with your broker all your insurance needs. If the broker doesn't ask questions to ascertain your full needs analysis, as required by the province, then run the other way!

Third, ask as many questions as you need to feel fully informed. This is not the time to feel timid or too embarrassed to admit you don't know something, or that things sound complicated. Insurance should be straight forward and simple. If your broker is making it too complicated maybe s/he shouldn't be your broker.

Fourth, avoid the hit-and-runs. An agent who is only interested in selling you a product and does not talk about meeting with you to discuss an overall plan is likely not someone looking after all your insurance or financial needs. Ask your agent about his/her process when sitting down with a client. How frequent will your meetings be and what will be the objectives of those meetings? Once comfortable, you can decide from there if this is someone with whom you would like to have a long-term professional relationship.

Mortgage protection is just the beginning. Insurance is for life and the living. So, though *buyer beware* is the rule here, I say *buyer seize control* and know what truly protects you, your family, and your lives.

ABOUT THE AUTHOR

Born in Montreal and raised in
Toronto, Edith Kernerman has been
an entrepreneur since the age of 14
when she opened up her own art
school in North Toronto. Having
lived in New York and London,
Kernerman has made Toronto her
home as she built a variety of small
businesses and organizations, both
for profit and not-for profit, and
some with international standing
in the medical field.

Kernerman's work has consistently centred around education—in art, in lactation, and now in finance. There has always been a recurring theme of educating people to achieve their own goals in each of these fields. Whether it was about helping new artists on a technical level or teaching artists how to teach; helping mothers and families with their breastfeeding goals or coaching lactation consultants how to work in the field of lactation medicine. This theme has been prevalent in and continues to dominate Kernerman's work in the financial field since she first became life licensed in 2014.

Currently, Kernerman works both as a financial advisor to business owners, professionals, and young families, while mentoring other agents and advisors in the field of Financial Services. Kernerman co-founded FiduSure Financial with the goal of designing a unique and extraordinary platform on which agents and advisors could create their dream business in the financial services world. More importantly, those business ideas *could be fulfilled without ever having to compromise on ethics, money, or putting client priorities above all else—because those priorities align so clearly with FiduSure's vision. FiduSure's three-pronged approach of Wealth Accumulation, Wealth Preservation, and Tax Minimization are the cornerstone of their work with both clients and advisors.*

Edith Kernerman has her Mutual Fund Registration, Branch Designation, and is Life Licensed. She is also an International Board Certified Lactation Consultant. She is the mother of three children.

Notes:

Notes:

PREPARING FOR THE
3D REAL ESTATE DISRUPTION
Ted Tsiakopoulos

ACKNOWLEDGEMENT

This chapter is dedicated to my wife, Soula, and son, George. Soula, thank you for holding down the fort while I wrote this chapter and your interesting insights

George, your spirit, and curiosity keep me on my toes. Never change. I hope you can use these strategies in the future to become successful

A thank you to Joelle Hamilton for making me sound a little cooler than I really am.

My thoughts and prayers go out to those impacted by the recent pandemic

INTRODUCTION

When I was growing up, my parents always said – "prepare for the unexpected." Nothing rings truer today. The world is fighting a pandemic that will likely plunge the global economy into a recession if not worse. In these uncertain and tumultuous times, one thing is certain – the next decade will be very different from the last. Some have compared the next decade to the lost decades faced by the Japanese economy.

For financially-focused Gen Z who worry about becoming successful in the world, what will the next 10 years look like? The oldest (aged 24) are already graduating from college and university, entering the workforce, and will be buying or renting their first home. Those at the age of 15 should start to plan today. In general, this generation will be making some tough housing decisions for the first time in the next decade. But what economy will they be buying into? What challenges will they face? What skills will they need to be financially independent and resilient in the face of constant change? How can educators, realtors and builders play their part in setting them up for success in the housing market? This chapter is designed to answer these questions.

Global crisis aside, a 3D wave is coming and it's going to disrupt the real estate market. Growing **digitization**, growing household **debt** and aging **demographics** will change the economic landscape as we know it. De-globalization could be an additional "D" disruption. There is some evidence that de-globalization could become a long term reality given recent trade tensions and the impact the global pandemic could have on trust and global supply chains. All factors working together point to a modest pace of economic growth and less job security.

This chapter is written for Gen Z who are planning for the future, for the people that will be teaching them relevant skills, for the real estate agents who'll help them along the way and for the builders, city planners and community that will shape how communities get built. Sprinkled throughout are some tips to help you prepare for the 3D wave.

If we've learned anything by what's going on in the world, it's that we should expect the unexpected. What follows is not what *will* happen, but rather what *could* happen.

Author's notes:

- When talking about Gen Z, the use of the words you/your and they/there are used interchangeably in this chapter.

- Gen Z means anyone born between 1996 and 2010.

- Disruptions cited in this report are not meant to be exhaustive

- The opinions expressed are those of the author and do not represent those of his employer. Views contained herein are for information only. Opinions expressed should not be construed as financial or investment advice. Please consult a licensed financial advisor who can assist you with your financial goals and asses your tolerance for risk.

THE DIGITAL ECONOMY DISRUPTION

Ted's Top Tips: Prepare for the unexpected

Digitization is the first element in the 3D wave. In this section, we'll define the digital economy and give a little background on how it was born. I will also explore the impacts it will have on labour markets and Gen Z, and present the important role that educators and realtors can play in setting this generation up for financial success.

What is the digital economy?

We're currently in what many experts call the fourth industrial revolution, aka the birth of the digital economy.[1] I know what you're thinking, what's the digital economy? According to The Canadian Encyclopedia, "the digital economy is the economic activity conducted through digital technologies such as the Internet."[2] Put simply, it's the economic activity generated by billions of online connections among people, businesses, machines, data, and processes.[3]

In 2017, Statistics Canada found that the gross domestic product connected to the digital economy represented 5.5% of Canada's total economic activity.[4] That's $109.7 billion!

From 2010 to 2017, the nominal GDP of digital economic activities (+40.2%) grew faster than the overall economy (+28.0%). This growth is proof that digitization is disrupting

---

[1]   Schwab, Klaus - "The Fourth Industrial Revolution" (2016)
[2]   The Canadian Encyclopedia. 2019. "Canada and the Digital Economy" (2020)
[3]   Deloitte - "What is the digital economy? – Unicorns, transformation and the internet of things." (2020)
[4]   Statistic Canada - "Measuring digital economic activities in Canada, 2010 to 2017 (2019)

Canada's economy. But, how will it impact the labour and real estate markets? How do we plan for it? Let's take a look!

How we got here

To better understand where we're going and prepare for the unexpected, we have to understand where we came from. Before digitization, the world was transformed by three industrial revolutions. The first began in England between 1760 and 1850 with the advent of urban manufacturing thanks to hydro power and steam engines, which made it possible to use machines instead of human labour. The second started in the United States in 1870, which popularized mass production via the first real assembly lines. This era is also known for popularizing the first communication technologies (the telegraph, the telephone, and radio), making it possible to share news, ideas, and information faster. The third started with the invention of the computer chip in 1961, dubbed the "silicon chip." By 1969, we put a man on the moon. Today, virtually everyone has a cell phone and most households have a computer or laptop.

Like the last three revolutions, digitization will disrupt labour markets, increase supply, keep inflation and interests low, and increase debt.[5]

<u>Labour market impacts</u>

Way back in 1995, Don Tapiscott, who coined the phrase "digital economy," made a number of predictions that he felt the digital economy would bring. He predicted that "so-called middlemen jobs connecting customers to products would either improve or go extinct."[6] And, he was right.

---

[5] Bank of Canada - "Managing the Fourth Industrial Revolution" (2019)
[6] Tapiscott, Don - "The Digital Economy: Promise and Peril in the Age of Networked Intelligence" (1995)

Digitization will continue to have wide-ranging implications on the labour market. New technologies have been and are being developed at lightning speeds. New advancements in AI, big data, and machine learning are fueling the rise of automation, for both routine and non-routine tasks. Some occupations will grow, others will be created, and some will become redundant.

To control costs and mitigate the squeeze on profits from a slower growing economy, companies will continue to modernize equipment and processes by investing in digital technologies. This could shift the production process from labour-intensive to capital-intensive.

The general consensus is that between 40-50% of jobs could be disrupted in the next decade. While new jobs will be created in the IT sector, the speed at which workers will be displaced will far outpace the economy's ability to replace impacted jobs[7]. On net, this disruption will be negative and lead to chronic unemployment that persists over time. Roles that could be most disrupted are jobs that are more task-oriented which include: clerical or administrative roles, call centre jobs, retail and tourism, financial, and transportation to name a few. I'll discuss this in more detail below (see *how educators can help*).

<u>What this means for Gen Z</u>

In the future, workers will be armed with better tools to do their work and their productivity should increase. Meaning it will take them less time to do their job, negatively impacting the average hours worked per week. With a shorter work week, Gen Z craving financial stability may need to diversify their employment options, beyond one employer. If the decreasing average hours worked per week in North America[8] since the 1970s is any indication, this downward trend will continue to gain momentum in the

---

[7]   Horizons Canada, MARS (2020)
[8]   Statistics Canada Labour Force Survey

foreseeable future. This means the gig[9] economy will only grow in size. This coupled with the prospect of earning less than generations before them, will challenge their ability to be financially independent.

Now, it's time to talk about the elephant in the room – housing affordability. We've seen the headlines about the housing affordability crisis in Toronto and Vancouver and about how homeownership is just a pipe dream for many young Canadians. We also know that rental vacancy rates in Toronto, while inching higher in 2019[10], are still near historic lows. My view is that incomes will be hard-pressed to keep pace with higher rents and house prices, particularly if ownership and rental supply doesn't respond to price signals in a timely way.

It is true that economic downturns, like the one we're living today, could dampen prices and rents – resulting in some immediate relief. However, job losses and declines in income are also prevalent. In fact, incomes adjust faster given the stickiness of prices and rents in a downturn.

Rental and housing affordability are reaching a tipping point and more needs to be done to face this challenge head on. Educators, realtors, and builders all have a part to play in positioning Gen Z for success.

---

[9]   A Gig economy is comprised of *Gig* workers that are independent contractors, online platform workers, contract firm workers, on-call workers and temporary workers. *Gig* workers enter into formal agreements with *on-demand* companies, for example Uber or Task Rabbit, to provide services to the company's clients.

[10]   Canada Mortgage and Housing Corporation, Renter Market Reports (2020)

How educators can help

Ted's Top Tips: Integrate essential future skills into current curriculum

John F. Kennedy coined the phrase - "Ask not what your country can do for you, ask what you can do for your country". Educators at all levels, be it elementary, secondary or higher education, are uniquely positioned to help Gen Z prepare for the digitization disruption by teaching them the right skills and strategies. Below, are the two things educators can act on.

<u>Career planning</u>

As I mentioned earlier, some jobs will be enhanced by automation, others will be created, and the rest will be replaced. By understanding how technology will impact occupations and which ones will be most and least susceptible to it, educators can help the next generation take control of their careers early.

Problem solvers that use critical thinking particularly in the IT space, people leaders, mediators, health care and other specialized consultants are broad skill sets that will be most resilient to automation. Meaning jobs that require creativity, negotiation, persuasion emotional and social intelligence, and a connection to people will be complimented by technology and not substituted.

Occupations that are more susceptible to automation are those that are founded in routine and don't involve a high-level of social skills. To remain relevant, Gen Z working in these fields will need to be able to use their digital savvy to innovate and create the tasks of the future.

Below is a breakdown of the occupations that are most and least susceptible to automation.

MOST SUSCEPTIBLE	LEAST SUSCEPTIBLE
<ul><li>Logistics and transportation</li><li>Office and administrative support</li><li>Factory, sales, and service jobs that do not involve high-level social skills</li><li>Select building trades (*i.e.*, bricklayers)</li></ul>	<ul><li>Jobs in education</li><li>Non-diagnostic health care, like doctors, nurses, dentists, therapists, psychologists</li><li>Law enforcement</li><li>Management</li><li>Mediation and consultancy</li><li>Business, finance, marketing</li><li>Sports</li><li>Arts</li><li>Mathematics, science, engineering</li></ul>

Table 1 - Source: Bank of Canada, The Digital Economy:
Bank of Canada Review, spring 2017, MARS, Horizons Canada

Financial Literacy

Financial skills are also important for both personal and career development. Few elementary and high school programs across the country include financial education as part of the curriculum[11]. Basics of how the economy works, budgeting, savings and investing are not all mandatory course topics covered in the curriculum in a holistic manner although some progress has been made recently. This is problematic, especially if we hope to put a dent in the alarming growth of household debt in Canada. It's never too early to learn financial literacy basics.

Canadian teens rank relatively well in overall global financial literacy scores[12] but score lower on more basic questions pertaining to the value of savings and how interest rates work. A recent *Federal Consumer Agency of Canada* survey

---

[11] Corporate Research Associates – "An Overview of Financial Literacy in Canada" (2016)

[12] OECD Financial Literacy Survey

found that households have trouble distinguishing between the amortization and term of a mortgage. They also don't understand how compound interest works. If our job is to prepare the next generation, that's not cool! Moreover, empirical data suggests that financial education will decrease Gen Z's likelihood of defaulting[13] on a loan. So, both households and lenders benefit.

Gen Z is the most connected generation and technology is ingrained in their daily activities. Educators at all levels should explore how to best leverage digital technology and use it to create financial literacy programs that educate, engage, and inform. It's our job to give young Canadians the tools they need to make the right financial decisions.

How realtors can help

Ted's Top Tip: Realtors need to better manage client needs versus wants

Some of the more traditional functions of a realtor have been displaced by technology. What hasn't changed is the value realtors add to the home buying process. Although technology can help package data for buyers to help inform decision making, some buyers don't have the experience and intuition necessary to accurately analyze data and act on it. More importantly, buyers and sellers may not have the capacity to negotiate the best price in volatile markets.

To say that we live in uncertain economic times is an understatement. Buyers and sellers will increasingly need to leverage a realtor's expertise to participate in the housing market. In fact, many already are. Recent survey[14] results indicate that 78% of recent home buyers leveraged the services of a realtor in 2019, up sharply from 61% in 2018.

---

[13]   US Federal Reserve Board
[14]   CMHC Mortgage Consumer Survey (2019)

With housing affordability challenges and the threat of relying on multiple sources of income to make ends meet, realtors will play a key role. Realtors in partnership with lenders can help manage Gen Z's expectations by helping them make more rational housing decisions, ones based on their budgets and needs, not on their wants. Finding a home that is affordable, that meets the space and transit needs of a household have consistently ranked highest among buyer needs as indicated in the figure below.

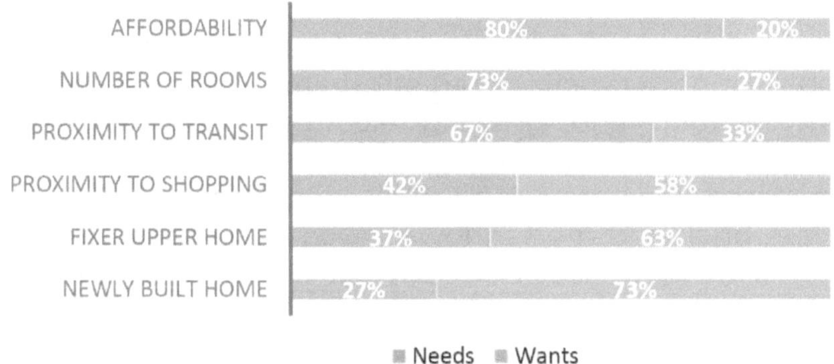

Source: CMHC Mortgage and Consumer Survey, 2019

Ted's Top Tips: Adopt the latest technologies

While you're mastering the art of helping clients make rational decisions, don't forget to stay on top of and adopt the latest digital tools. Gen Z will expect you to give virtual video tours via social media and provide them with digital information that is packaged in a way to provide deeper insights[15] that they can act on immediately. So, keep your eyes peeled for software advances because you'll need them to better serve your tech-savvy clients in the future.

---

[15]   Giraffe Realty

The second element of the 3D wave is debt. Debt is a dirty word in some circles, but Gen Z has to understand how it impacts their short-term and long-term financial stability. They have to learn how to foster a healthy relationship with debt by implementing winning debt strategies now. Their ability to buy or rent a home in the future depends on it.

A history on debt – how did we get here?

The post 1995 period was characterized by increasing globalization, a synchronized effort among central banks to fight inflation and growing electronic commerce. The *"Amazon effect"* is a good example of how electronic commerce transformed the retail experience - contributing to less brick and mortar, lower fixed costs for businesses and the ability to pass these savings onto consumers in the form of lower prices. These post 1995 events were responsible for restraining wage pressures, consumer prices and inflation while providing more stable conditions within which investors, businesses and consumer decisions could be made. So clearly some important benefits to the economy were realized. However, there were also some unintended consequences. With interest rates trending lower, there was less of an incentive to save and more incentive to add to household debt. Indeed, savings rates peaked in the 1980s. The figure below illustrates the impact that lower interest rates had on savings and debt since the 1980s. Today, Toronto and Vancouver households are heavily indebted[16] relative to their global counterparts.

---

[16]   Statistics Canada, Equifax Canada

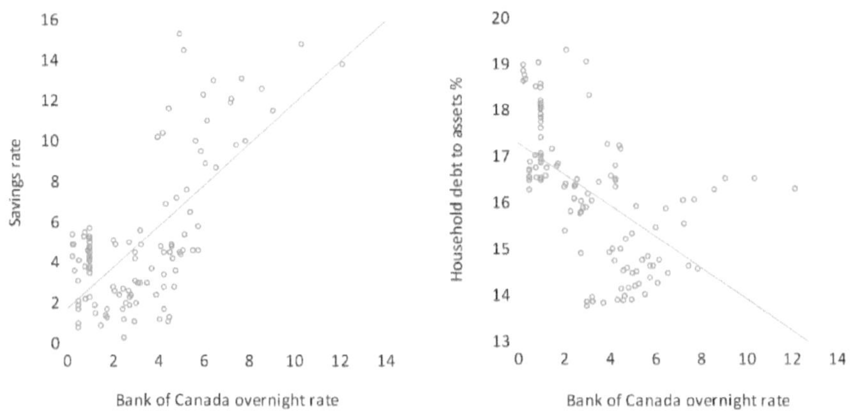

Source: Statistics Canada, Bank of Canada

All debts are not created equal

Not all debts are created equal – some are good and some are bad. **Good debts** increase your net worth or create future value, like a student loan or residential mortgage. This type of debt reduces your debt to asset ratio. **Bad debts** typically put on a credit card are created when you buy consumer goods that depreciate in value.   This has the opposite effect of increasing your debt to asset ratio.

Debt and wealth strategies

Ted's Top Tips: Manage the level of interest rates

At the time of writing, policy makers were fighting the global COVID-19 pandemic by slashing interest rates and increasing government spending in hopes of avoiding a more serious economic downturn. While this stimulus may boost inflation and interest rates down the road, it is unlikely to reverse the long term downtrend in interest rates. While the traditional savings life cycle model argues that it is completely rational for Gen Z to borrow more and save less when young and earning less income, too much of a good thing is never healthy. So it is prudent to boost savings in good economic times to provide a "piggy bank" that one can tap into during bad economic times or when income is disrupted. The current pandemic highlights how difficult it is to manage risk when saving less and living paycheque to paycheque. This means, reign in the temptation to borrow more when interest rates are falling. Financial planners suggest saving at least 10% of gross income as a rule of thumb. I would suggest saving 20-25% in good economic times for that rainy day.

If you have succeeded in saving enough, consider a variable rate mortgage when buying a home especially if you can tolerate fluctuations. Why? Eight times out of ten, you would have been better off historically. But take it one step further. Not only should you tie the mortgage to the variable rate but try tying your payment to a fixed mortgage rate schedule. This will not only force you to pay down debt and build equity faster, it will help you manage interest rate risk should rates move in the opposite direction.

Ted's Top Tips: Channel savings into the investment market

Downward trending interest rates during uncertain times have traditionally been lucrative for those channelling savings into bond and stock markets[17]. Diversifying your portfolio by Investing in longer term government bonds, companies providing utilities, consumer staples such as health, food and pharmaceutical companies has proven to be a wise decision during periods of uncertainty. For those with a higher risk tolerance, investing a small share of your portfolio in the gold sector may also hedge against lower interest rates, depreciating global currencies or higher inflation. But lower interest rates also make "blue chip" dividend paying stocks quite attractive as an alternative to low interest bearing investments such as GICs or T-bills. Thankfully, a tax free savings account (TFSA) is a great product to not only shelter investment gains from taxation but also allow the flexibility of holding stocks, bonds, mutual

---

17   Stockcharts.com

funds under one umbrella. Tax free compounding over a number of years can help Gen Z accumulate a nest egg for rental payments or a down payment on a home purchase.

Ted's Top Tips: Create a budget and stick to it!!

The foundation for financial freedom starts with a budget. Forget about having any luck with saving, investing and managing debt if you do not have a budget. My mom, the CFO of our household many years ago, taught me how to budget at age 10 when she pulled out a pen and quickly scribbled something on her dinner napkin at dinner one night. Having lived through wars, the Great Depression, a few recessions, and having nothing but the clothes on their back when they immigrated to Canada, my parents understood the importance of not spending more than income earned. That night, my mom was keeping track of what she'd spent on dinner. While the boomer generation was criticized for not living their lives, for me it was a blunt message on how to strike a balance between savings and consumption.

Did you know that the majority of Canadians don't have a budget?[18] As someone who started saving at 15 when I got my first job, this boggles my mind. Here's what I learned in high school that changed my perspective on things:

1. Resources are scarce – we have to make choices and trade-offs[19]

2. Income is a constraint and binding[20]

This is why you need to create a monthly budget and make a clear distinction between what you need and what you want, so you can live within your means. Also, steer clear of

---

[18] Federal Consumer Agency of Canada – Financial Capability Survey
[19] Fernbach, Kan, Lynch – "Squeezed: Coping with Constraint through Efficiency and Prioritization" (2015)
[20] Fernbach, Kan, Lynch – "Squeezed: Coping with Constraint through Efficiency and Prioritization" (2015)

the biggest budget killers – peer pressure, keeping up with latest tech devices, and emotionally-driven purchases. I usually convert what I consider emotionally charged purchases to how many labour hours I am giving up on that purchase. This helped control my emotions which psychologists suggest is key to making rational decisions. Try it!!

When should you start budgeting? As early as you can. Starting early means you'll master the right budgeting habits before real life hits and you have a car loan, student loan, a mortgage and two kids in daycare.

The *Federal Consumer Agency of Canada* just released a great budgeting tool to get you started – it's called the "FCAC Budget Planner." Use it!

The bottom line – Creating a budget and sticking to it forces you to live within your means and allows you to save and stay/get out of debt. This means you'll be able to build wealth at a younger age.

Ted's Top Tips: Build equity as soon as you can

When you buy a home, your bank or lender will give you a residential mortgage. This is considered "good" debt because it allows you to build equity (aka, wealth). The more equity you have, the better off you'll be financially.

When you own a home, you're building equity in two ways:

1. By paying down your debt: you own a little more of your home with every mortgage payment

2. The value of your home grows over time and is worth more than what you paid for it

Ted's Top Tips: Build wealth while you rent

Owning a home is one way to build wealth, but you can also do it while renting or living at home. If the rent you're paying is less than what you'd pay on a mortgage payment, you can channel those savings into building a solid financial portfolio with diversified assets, like stocks, bonds, and mutual funds. Again, this takes discipline and the presence of mind to have a budget.

Ted's Top Tips: More choices for aging households = more choices for Gen Z

As mentioned at the outset, builders, city planners and the community also have a shared responsibility to set Gen Z up for success. How? By promoting more choice.

While the world's population is aging particularly in Europe and Japan, Canada will not be immune to this trend. By 2030, households over the age of 65 will comprise over 20 per cent[21] of Toronto's population. This ratio is 50 per cent higher than the previous decade and represents the maturing of the younger and older boomer generation.

Households may be aging but they are also living longer. As a result, aging in place will only accelerate. History has shown that about 80% of households over the age of 65 [22] age in place and refrain from leaving their existing residence. Given that most aging households live in low-rise housing, this will only further restrict housing options for younger buyers looking for space in the next decade.

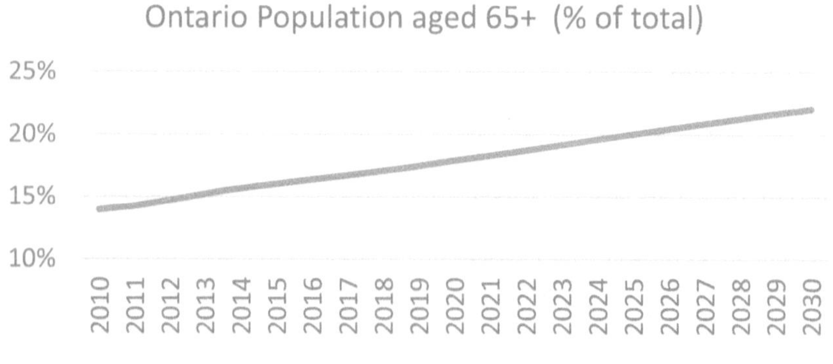

Source: Statistics Canada Census, author projections post 2016

---

[21]   Statistics Canada Census, CMHC estimates
[22]   Statistics Canada Census

What really matters for boomer households is living in a community that they are familiar with that provides amenities that will be important to them such as transit, retail and medical services. Many of Toronto's yellow belt[23] communities boast not only the amenities that seniors need but also the capacity to intensify further.

Remember my mother`s lesson on budgeting during dinner time in the 1970s? Well my folks still live in the same single detached home they purchased in the 1970s and craving alternative living arrangements. More mid to higher density housing will not only provide seniors with more maintenance free housing choices in their existing communities, but will also entice more listings and choices for generation Z as seniors vacate their existing space. To make this happen, we must embrace and promote collaboration between builders, city planners and the community.

Ted's Top Tips: Leverage technology to manage an aging workforce and rising costs

The building industry needs to change the conversation from housing construction to housing production. The fact is that most home builders in North America, including here in Toronto, build homes the same way they did 50 years ago. The speed of innovation and productivity growth[24] in the construction industry has lagged behind other industries in Canada over the past decade. This needs to change particularly given the opportunities that advances in technology will offer over the next decade.

First and foremost, leveraging technology will help alleviate accelerating labour shortages, owing to an aging population, over the next decade. Secondly, by manufacturing pre-fabricated parts in an offsite facility and

---

23   Yellow belt neighbourhoods are zoned exclusively for single detached homes

24   Statistics Canada – Multi factor productivity, productivity accounts

shipping parts to a building site for final assembly - this will help boost productivity, and reduce productions costs. Lower productions costs will restrain price increases and provide more affordable options for Gen Z residents. But automating production does come with challenges. You need enough production capacity to ensure the upfront capital costs to build a manufacturing plant remain financially feasible.

It is reassuring to see some home builders having adopted these building practices successfully especially in Sweden, Australia and Asia. Closer to home, a few Toronto based companies manufacture different home panels and use robotics for final assembly before shipping parts to local job sites. Similarly, *Sidewalk Labs* in Toronto is also proposing factory based construction as part of its waterfront development plan[25].

Conclusion

The recent pandemic is a stark reminder of the uncertain times we live in. Preparing as best as we can for the 3D disruption will be the difference between success and failure. We all have a shared responsibility to guide the next generation along a path of success. We also have the luxury of history on our side. Identifying best practices that worked over time while staying clear of practices that didn't can help achieve better results. The courage of front line workers fighting the current pandemic tells me we will remain resilient in the face of future change. Best wishes to all including Gen Z.

Your thoughts and questions are always welcomed. Feel free to reach me at the email address below.

---

[25]   Sidewalk Labs – *"Toronto Tomorrow: A New Approach for Inclusive Growth"(2019)*

ABOUT THE AUTHOR

Ted Tsiakopoulos is a professional economist and sought after speaker with over 25 years of experience analyzing housing and financial markets. Ted has also worked as an investment counsellor on Bay Street. His analytical toolkit includes experience with both fundamental and technical analysis. Over his professional career, his commentary and research has been widely quoted across major media outlets such as Money Magazine, BNN, CTV and CBC. Ted has devoted significant personal time to financial literacy research and education serving as chair for a number of financial literacy committees and as a consultant to Junior Achievement of Canada. Ted is currently on the Board of Directors for the Toronto Association for Business and Economics, member of the Canadian Association for Business and Economics and a member of the LAI Land Economics Association.

Ted can be reached at ttsiakop@cmhc.ca

Notes:

Notes:

LIFE BRINGS US TO MANY PLACES. LOVE BRINGS US HOME

Melina Zeppieri

"Hi John, how are you?" "Great Mary, how is the market?"

"Hi Sara, haven't seen you in ages. How are you doing?" 'Hi Mary, not bad. How is the market?"

"Hi Claude, lovely day. How are you?" "Hi Mary, can't complain. How is the market?"

"Hi Connie, nice to hear from you." "Oh Mary, I can't believe it. I heard last night on City Pulse that condo prices are going through the roof. Tell me, how is the market?"

I can't believe, in a given day, the number of times the question, *"How is the market?"* becomes the opener of a potentially engaging conversation. Perhaps, for those, whom you have met for the first time, the brokerage pin flashing on your left lapel is a giveaway. For those, whom you have shared many a cup of coffee, they simply value your opinion.

However, herein lies the challenge. You could simply reply with one of the illustrious adjectives like amazing, phenomenal, unbelievable, astounding, and impressive, to site a few. You could hand over TRREB's Market Year-in-Review and Outlook Report, the printed statistics in summary form, which any of the respective boards have diligently prepared, detailing time frame, type of home, listing price, selling price, inventory on hand, percentile community comparisons and more. You could even reply with a question. *"What would you like to know?"*

Regardless of how you choose to address the question, *"How is the market?"* one pertinent element prevails. Although you know, you have routinely reviewed, analysed and pondered their very same query, the answer however does not lie in a one size fits all.

Let's stop to think for a moment. Would your reply to John, the engineer who married your friend Lucy's daughter and lives in the charming 2 bedroom freehold townhome, you sold them 2 years ago, be the same as the one you would give to Sara, Maria's youngest daughter, renting a condo 40 mins from her mother's home. Currently a fitness instructor, dealing with the aftermath of a lengthy divorce proceeding, all you know of Sara is that she is bitter with the world.

Or, how about your reply to Claude, whom you briskly pass on your walk every day, as you both go in opposite directions enjoying the morning breeze. He owns the captivating 2 acres property just inside the gatehouse of the rural community of King, complete with landscaped grounds, outdoor kitchen and a pool that would fare above those in any of the resorts.

Then there is Connie, ready to sell her house today, ready to stay where she is tomorrow, picking up news in bits and pieces, from here and there. She has the art of drawing conclusions that are totally unfound and is always in a state of panic, listening to anyone prepared to listen to her.

Without doubt your approach will not, cannot, nor should be identical. Let us consider a recent quote from TRREB* President Michael Collins [Globe News Wire, March 02, 2020] "Robust regional economic conditions, strong population growth and low borrowing costs will support increased home sales in 2020. Market conditions will become tighter, as transactions will continue to outpace the growth in available listings. The resulting increase in competition between buyers will likely result in an acceleration in price growth across all major market segments."

Words, well-articulated obviously conveying a concise analogy of where we currently stand and the variables affecting the current and future real estate market, supported with summary tables, conveniently downloadable from TRREB.ca As resourceful as these statistics may be, when delivering the message to those whom we meet, the key lies in how little or how much is relevant to our actual audience. Each encounter is unique.

- What is their particular situation?

- Who are the players?

- What are their challenges?

- Is there a sense of urgency?

- Is there a sense of hesitancy?

[*The Toronto Regional Real Estate Board is Canada's largest real estate board with more than 56,000 residential and commercial professionals connecting people, property and communities."]

When we learn to listen to what is being said and often more importantly to what is not being said, we learn to identify underlying concerns, issues that may induce a form of anguish. It is our role to provide a viable solution that will both assist them, create a credulous environment and earn their respect.

Having an affinity to the aging population, this demographic has been of prime personal concern.

Perhaps, the numerous years spent volunteering for one of the senior residences, allowed me to experience first-hand their unique dilemmas.

Perhaps, my upbringing as a child of immigrant parents prepared me to exercise certain sensitivities.

Perhaps, a simple curiosity to understand their frustrations and the need to improve their situation were all the basis of this innate desire to improve the important communication skill of listening.

Supporting our elderly as they navigate this new stage of Life begins with communication. The question *"How is the market?"* takes on an entirely different dimension, as does, the approach to initiating the conversation.

For siblings and adult children, it is often a challenge to understand what their parents are going through. It is difficult to comprehend that they are looking at a more wrinkled and possibly a less capable version of the Mom and Dad they knew and are at a loss, as to what they need to do, how to do it and when would be the right time. They are overwhelmed with their own obligations, that they may overlook the idea of building a partnership with the services of qualified professionals.

As a Senior Real Estate Specialist [ASA@ Accredited Seniors Agent designation], we take pride in holding their hand, working with the family dynamics, the existing circumstances and possible solutions, all while facilitating a transitioning period that suits the patrimony.

Coming to terms with their losses and holding on to all that remains, older people are engaged in trying to comprehend what their life has meant and the memories that will live on when they are no longer here. They may be fragile. They may be hurting. They may be lonely, isolated or are simply dealing with a life that is now burdened with a disillusioned heart. They may be in optimal health and are looking at ways to enjoy life's beautiful gifts. With the compassion and understanding of those around them, coming to terms with one's legacy becomes less daunting.

As the voice in the process, we can make the difference between lonely, frustrating, complex years or alternatively, years that are simplistic, rewarding and tranquil amidst the changes, for both the parents and their children. The examples are many....

One morning, after my routine walk, I actually sat down on the bench under the Weeping Willow tree, that marked one of the entrances to the park, soaking up the rays of sunshine that enveloped the skies. Minutes later Claude, at the tail end of his run, joined me. After the usual small talk, I came to understand that Claude, had been a financial consultant and as of two and a half years ago, had retired. His wife, Monique, would be a retiring in the upcoming month of June from a long-standing career as a high school principal. He was excited about new possibilities for them to share.

Although they loved their home and had hosted many grandioso events for family and friends, their 'bucket list' still held many dreams to be fulfilled. Boasting optimal health and vigorous energy, plans for world travel, of places far and exotic, in the spring and fall months of the year were a priority. Ironic that they too had fast approached the fall season of their lives. The usual winters, on the oceanside beaches of Florida, now ranked third place in their plans. Of equal importance was the finding of a Muskoka Lakes chalet to relax during the summers surrounded by their children, growing grandchildren and their dear friends. They were decisive about their options, knowing a move to Condo-Living would be their first step. With no mortgage payments and pension funds, in part, that would address their monthly maintenance fee and taxes, our focus remained on selecting a suitable condo.

Their search for a modern classic building, emanating the elegance and craftsmanship that they had been accustomed to, played 'front row centre' in their choice. Furthermore, they paid particular attention to the details and functional layout of the suite. Luxurious rooftop patio and state-of-the-art fitness centre made for the perfect combination in refined lifestyle amenities. With distinct wants identified, geographic proximity to the neighbourhood that currently housed their married children and their families, became the needle in the haystack. Perseverance, guided suggestions and few constraints of time frame, opened the door to numerous possibilities and the perfect condo was soon a reality.

By contrast, John, the young engineer, at the onset of his career and Sophia, the love of his life had lived on the outskirts of the city for a few short years. Although, the new executive townhome had served them well until now, the coming of their first child and being closer to her parents left Sophia with anxiety and turmoil. Her thoughts were in constant conflict, as she struggled with what would be the ultimate solution.

They could convert John's home office to a cute and comfy nursery. Whimsical patterns on the wall and a soft grey carpet below the antique rocker would definitely add the finishing touches and change the feel of the room. But dreams of the 4 Bedroom ranch style bungalow on a ravine lot where not only their first born but their growing family would be proud to call home, played havoc with decision making. They battled with the knowledge that the market showed a significant increase in value in their townhome and potentially made for a lucrative return on their investment. They had also analysed the costs of moving closer to the core of the city, in a charming, mature neighbourhood but worried about the implications of having to carry a mortgage.

Even Sophia's parents had offered the use of the east wing of their ancestral home, complete with its own entrance and in close proximity to work for both her and John.

For them the questions, do we stay and renovate, do we move in with parents or do we move into a larger home were going to be more of a personal preference rather than one that made market sense. Given their busy schedules, doing the leg work and providing them with options and a round table discussion, with the in-laws, made the decision process, a concrete one, that balanced both the pro and cons long term. The hunt for the home of their dreams in Edenbridge Humber Valley was underway.

Connie, my dear Connie, on the other hand, was a challenge. She too had retired from a teaching position and lived in Fonthill, a residential suburb laden with fruit orchards and only 12 miles from Niagara Falls. Her eldest son, Jake an honour student in journalism, on the hunt for a permanent position, had unexpectedly been given termination papers. Due to increased online sales, public attendance steadily declined at the show room he managed part-time and the owners had decided to do away with the storefront. Her youngest daughter Cynthia had recently returned to college to secure her degree in nursing. As a single mom and with two little ones, concentrating on her studies was challenging and she too had decided to move in with Grandmother Connie. Even Connie's mother Rosalie lived with them and with a kidney disorder was in treatment three times a week as an out-patient, at the Niagara Health Well and Site. Every time Connie and I spoke, it was apparent she was overwhelmed with the conditions at home. Thoughts of putting her mom in a retirement home, although offering some medical relief, constantly anguished her. She wanted to be the one, to care for her mother but she also had an obligation to her daughter and the two little ones, Samantha and Noah. Now with Jake back in his quarters in the basement, Cynthia and Jake clashed over who was taking advantage of whom.

In desperation, Connie contemplated selling everything and giving them each the funds they needed to make fresh starts on their own. The fear, of dealing with dear Rosalie and the possibility of others tucking her in bed at night tormented her. Hence, the meetings or phone calls with Connie were never consistent in thought and being of assistance translated into the listening ear, which today was of prime importance and tomorrow could prove to be more so.

Not only do our everyday encounters differ from casual to significant, the complexity of the circumstances and the role players present themselves like the protagonists in the intriguing scenes of a four-act play.

I recall meeting for the first time with Maria, a widowed mother of six married children, as she shook her head, and spoke in a feeble voice about not knowing where she was going to go without 'her Giuseppe'. Her health was clearly deteriorating yet with sound mind, she would easily drift into storytelling mode. She spoke of how they had found this *'bella casetta'* beautiful, little house when she and her husband Giuseppe were first married and how they were the envy of the family because they took that gem and made it into a home. *"Giuseppe was a good man. He never stop work, to buy all this custom furniture too and I make every drape you see on the windows. We never go nowhere. Maybe just once in a while."*

As I sit there with her son, Andrea, he mumbles 'oh here she goes again". In reality, his mother is engaged in the review process of her life, whether consciously or unconsciously. Like the pages in her wedding album, she is trying to understand her legacy. She recalls working hard and making sacrifices along the road and now as she contemplates having to leave this house for good, all those memories are overbearing. I explain to Andrea and also his sister Sara, who has joined us, that their mother is not defying them, pretending to behave irrationally or listening with deaf ears as they put it. In actuality, she is simply learning to deal with it.

Often, adult children tend to be in the dark about their parent's behaviour or draw the wrong conclusions. It is hard to understand the person their mother has become. What happened to the loving, carefree woman, that the minute they came through the door would throw her arms around them, singing her all-time favourite tune *O Sole Mio*? For a moment, the almost real aroma of the biscotti she used to bake, seems to once again linger in the air. *"Vieni Tesoro...come my Treasure, so tell me Caterina was little Nicola good in class today or he give you trouble? You know I can fix everything."*

Memories of how she really did seem to 'fix everything' are so vivid and yet here we all sit, supposedly unable to 'fix nothing'. Is this the same mom they knew? Today, we are quick to assume the never-ending, senseless, repetitive conversations are being generalized as a sign of cognitive deterioration, when in reality they may simply be miscommunication.

In our fast-paced world, understanding and making time to spend with our seniors is a challenge in itself. As real estate professionals, it is our duty to *listen*. *Listen*, and *listen* even more. We must encourage them to reminisce and we must pay close attention to the seemingly irrelevant particulars, for in those same details, usually lie their deepest concerns.

That cup of tea that you graciously poured may be worth every ounce of its weight in gold. As for the aroma of mamas fresh baked biscotti, divine enjoyment, and a priceless gift. Neither, are in our mandate as realtors, but I prefer to think that they are a given, a personal touch, in the learning and engaging process.

Our everyday practice as realtors, commands asking questions, for we recognize that one question leads to another and the answers we receive are the missing pieces of the beautiful puzzle of a life well lived. I am consistently learning to build my own legacy, a comprehensive repertoire, through concrete advice and knowledgeable options gaining a clearer perspective on the brilliant lives of our seniors.

We have been taught well and our brokerages lend phenomenal support systems to allow us to excel in our field, ensuring details are not overlooked and that we have acted in the best interest of those whom we serve. In reality, working with our seniors goes far beyond the flawless paperwork in the transaction of a purchase or a sale.

Building trust and strong relationships are a priority; going beyond, translates into doing what someone else may choose not to. Providing them with an extensive network of experts who understand their unique needs and challenges, armed with resources to facilitate tasks, that allow them to make wise, calculated real estate decisions, may or may not translate into the sale or purchase of a property. The examples are many.

They may choose to 'age' in place, simply because they like their house; they like their friends next door; they like their neighbourhood; they like their local church; they like the little café` down the street and all their 'likes' are what they choose to keep. Perhaps, engaging in the services of a contractor providing minimal renovations will allow for improved accessibility.

With the continual emergence of innovative technologies and breakthroughs in the medical field, seniors not only are living longer but an elevated quality of life is within reach. [For detailed information and graphs see documented Statistics Canada reports]
https://www120.statcan.gc.ca/stcsr/en/sr1

Nursing homes that once mirrored sterile hospitals are no longer the only option. Many senior living communities now bask in state-of-the-art amenities and living quarters fully tailored to a resident's personal taste and style.

Downsizing and selecting a home in a community with facilities that allow for autonomy yet offering a more comprehensive or flexible option for care down the road, should their needs change over time is an ever growing want, the 'Perfect Sizing'.

Many choose to simply give up the family home. They are realistic about how increasingly difficult it is becoming to cut the lawn, shovel the snow, clean all the windows or repaint the kitchen.

Condo living is their reality, where the pressure of certain responsibilities falls in the hands of a management company.

By reassessing their position of home ownership and seeking the advice of an Accredited Senior Agent, the possibilities may differ. They may choose to travel more, add a weekend retreat to their portfolio or even a second home, away from home, beneath the sunny skies or shining stars of another land.

More and more are opting for a multi-generational scenario. There was a time, when immigrant families living under one roof was a cultural norm. Today, with an increasing demographic in Canada, the same holds true. Living with the in-laws, adult children moving back home, grandparents living with grandchildren or vice-versa grandchildren living with grandparents to facilitate their daily obligations, as housing prices and the cost of living escalates, make a multi-generational household an attractive option. It is no longer perceived a burden but rather a sign of gratitude, for that which, they can offer each other.

Lifestyle choices may vary but innovation in implementing a self-designed approach, a full spectrum of resources and the option of meeting personalized care, whether imminent or in the future, are a major FOCUS in the decision-making process, that we as ASA@, Accredited Senior Agents provide with the highest level of skill and professionalism, laced with genuine understanding and sensitivity.

The shift in our role becomes more comprehensive than the relationship of a client and his/her realtor. It often means co-ordinating the efforts of lawyers, estate planners, tax wizards, specialized lenders or reverse mortgage experts, executors and other family members. Forwarding a list of advisors, without having established a rapport with the various individuals or companies, identifying their strengths and/or weaknesses leaves suggesting suitable matches a compromising task rather than an enhancing experience.

As an ASA@, Accredited Senior Agent, we do not simply want to chase a listing or take a buyer from house to house. We pride ourselves in working as a consultant, hand in hand, with our seniors and the advisors they want to involve in the process.

Life transitions may be gradual or may be suddenly imposed due to a medical issue or other family crisis. Boomers, our largest demographics, may find themselves struggling with their own issues and those of their offspring or their aging parents.

Stressed? Relax. Bringing everyone to the table and recognizing their dilemma is a task we know well. The emotions, the situations and the dramatics are real. They are an expression of how one feels in that very moment. As paid negotiators, some with an MCNE@ designation [Master Certified Negotiation Expert], it is our responsibility to be consciously aware of those sentiments.

"Negotiating is deal making. We determine the needs of each side and then work on the puzzle of problem solving so that as many of those needs as possible are met. It's not about winning and losing but about getting a deal done that satisfies as many of the parties' needs, as possible. This happens through strategic information sharing, alignment of needs, sensitivity to emotions and psychology and mutual respect and trust."

~Suze Cumming,
The Nature of Real Estate I Blog January 30 2020

Following a few crucial but impactful steps from the onset will determine the tone for the outcome:

- Engage the parties in the decision making

- Allow each of them to voice what meets their needs; be considerate of the needs of others at the table

- Review the suggestions with an open mind, validating each of the possibilities

- Be aware of body language

- Discuss those options that are most feasible

- Reach a decision on merit rather than those that were most popular

- Narrow down the decision and re-evaluate the pros and cons

- Make a decisive choice and implement the decision with reassurance

One may say, that is logical. It is what we do all the time. Surprisingly, when emotions and family members share a seat around the same table, sound reasoning seems to get lost in the chatter. At the cost of hurtful arguments and sideshow comments, the ASA@ can skillfully manoeuvre the discussions and systematically prioritize the unresolved issues. In so doing, an execution plan is triggered and all present leave with a mandate in hand. Building a partnership with the services of qualified experts offsets the power struggles of family dynamics. No stress. No battles. No uncertainties. Simply the positive, supportive professionalism of those whom believe in finding the best solution, for all the players.

The Accredited Senior Agent, ASA@ designation awarded by Pivotal Aging Innovations Inc. was created to educate REALTORS@ in aspects of the real estate transaction that are specific to seniors. A better understanding of Canadian tax laws, estates and estate planning, wills and trusts, government grants and loans allow an ASA@ to work in a consulting capacity, with a network of professionals, excelling in their particular fields. Identifying skill sets and suggesting several recommendations for whom can best serve the needs of a senior, whether it be for them directly or extended family members facilitates the task of searching aimlessly for the proper fit. It may mean narrowing the options for contractors that can best complete the renovations, reputable in their service, with competitive quotes and select materials.

Diversely, it may entail setting an appointment with a lawyer to ensure their wishes are updated or speaking with the executor of an estate that has been appointed to deal with the wishes of the deceased person's estate.

Ultimately, minimizing their burden, with the resources we have at hand, increases the comfort level and builds the trust and respect we aspire to gain.

We often hear many speak of going above and beyond, of delivering the unexpected.

Is making the third trip to the same neighbourhood to see how it feels, going beyond?

Is finding a volunteer to help them sort the umpteen photos sitting in the shoe boxes, going above? Is helping them part with the six sets of china dishes they will no longer use or ensuring their prized cowboy hat is carefully wrapped and makes its way safely to the new hook on the condo wall really delivering more than is expected?

When we work from the heart, the results of our efforts are multi-fold. It is not about the things we were able to accomplish or the possible monies that we earned but rather the fulfillment in the process. We have no need to categorize our work, as going over and above. We have learned to listen to what has been said. We have learned to listen for what has not been said. We did the homework to find the answers. We even delivered the solutions. Yes, we may have achieved the goal we have set but the path to getting there has rewards in itself. The true riches lie in that wonderful journey. The experiences are bountiful. The relationships are priceless. The referrals are our lifeline. As for the trust and respect we have earned, validation of what we do has no greater measure.

"Trusting that in building and nurturing relationships, we are equally enriched."

MELINA ZEPPIERI, MCNE@; ASA@; ABR@; LUXE@
REAL ESTATE SALES PROFESSIONAL

ABOUT THE AUTHOR

MELINA ZEPPIERI, MCNE; ASA; ABR; LUXE;
REAL ESTATE SALES PROFESSIONAL
RE/MAX PREMIER INC.

MELINA is a dynamic, passionate visionary. As a seasoned, resourceful professional, her mandate is to identify the unique parameters of her clients and deliver on fulfilling their needs, consistently surpassing expectations and achieving customer service excellence.

As an accomplished entrepreneur in the GTA, with an accumulated 25 years of verifiable successes in hospitality and sales, steering growth and expansion are the trademarks of her high energy leadership qualities and infectious enthusiasm. Melina's focus has always been directed by sound morals, rendering her life, an intricate balance of work, family, spiritual well-being and self-development. She is a proud  mother of three adult children, professionals in their own rights, an elated 'nonna' to eight grandchildren, with an extensive portfolio of community involvement, including positions on the VCLA board of Villa Colombo Home for the Aged, the NCIC, National Congress of Italian Canadians in Toronto, the A.M.I.C.I., Association for the Memory of Italian Canadian Immigrants, the World Change Foundation and ICFF, Italian Contemporary Film Festival Event Co-ordinator. Honoured as a Dame Commander of Grace DCG, Sovereign Military Order of Saint John of Jerusalem Knights of Malta, she served as Secretary of Council for Prior Marko Mihic MD, KGCollar, for more than 18 years. Holding an OCT, Ontario College of Teaching degree, she enhanced her role in the classroom with providing English as a Second Language and adult preparation for Canadian Citizenship to members of the community. She is also fluent in both oral and written Italian.

A dedicated, relentless, results driven individual with exceptional interpersonal strengths, Melina will take care of finding your ideal home with all the essential criteria, inclusive of the neighbourhood amenities mattering most to you and your family. Equally, when selling your home, she will create a strategized and clearly defined marketing plan to attract potential buyers.

Whether negotiating the contract, recommending financial options or preparing the necessary documentation, be assured your closing for a purchase or a sale will be executed effectively, with a blend of persuasive, knowledgeable and proven methodologies.

Melina will often be heard saying "My most important asset is not **the property,** I am working with but rather, **the people,** whom own or display an interest in it."

Formal training and good standing membership with industry associations such as RECO, Real Estate Council of Ontario; CREA, Canadian Real Estate Association; OREA, Ontario Real Estate Association; and TRREB, Toronto Regional Real Estate Board all ensure we are accountable to our client but enrolling in specialized field trainings arms you with additional insight and a skillset that enriches the comprehension and expertise you lend those same clients....**the leading edge**. With an affinity to the aging population and their complex family components, Melina successfully engaged in both the **Accredited Seniors Agent @ [ASA] Pivotal** and **Accredited Buyers Representation @ [ABR]** programs, to be better equipped with current knowledge, in addition to issues and trends that affect the real estate industry.

In the interest of a positive outcome for all parties involved in the real estate transaction, negotiations play a vital role and a sound understanding of one's BATNA, a skill well learned in the **Master Certified Negotiation Expert@ [MCNE]** unique designation program, repeatedly serves Melina in the ongoing communications with both sides of a given transaction. Suze Cumming, the Canadian Director of the Real Estate Negotiation Institute@ facilitated the training that, upon completion, resulted in becoming "a part of an elite group of real estate professionals who are committed to serving their clients at the very highest level".

Recently, a study of the luxury homes market, verified that the selling or purchasing of an estate home did not fit the cookie cutter mold and attention to such properties required a specific, detailed process. The **Luxury Listing Specialist Designation [LUXE@]** has allowed Melina to gain a professional advantage when dealing with sellers of luxury properties. With a more comprehensive understanding of where to find prospective buyers and the insights on how to market the property appropriately, sets the tone for the unique blend of working with ease and passion.

Building and nurturing relationships on a foundation of TRUST and RESPECT is of significant importance to Melina, thereby fostering an environment of open communication and maximum support. With well-honed presentation skills, unparalleled professionalism and ethical standards, Melina brings a sound acumen and strong work ethic to her career. Constantly growing her sphere and enhancing her skills and training with personal development programs and accredited status, she maintains active roles in business conferences, networking and community events and strives to stay abreast of current local developments.

With a commanding presence, reflecting confidence, competence and charisma, Melina is instrumental in leading clients to live the **extraordinary life** they deserve in their **dream home**.

Make yours a reality. For a complimentary consultation boasting persona, understanding and vivid new horizons, meet with Melina.

Direct contact information: t. +1 647 400 0851 or via email melina.zeppieri@gmail.com

MELINA ZEPPIERI, MCNE; ASA; ABR; LUXE;
REAL ESTATE SALES PROFESSIONAL
RE/MAX PREMIER INC. BROKERAGE

9100 Jane Street
Building L, Suite 77
Vaughan, ON L4K 0A4
c. 647 400 0851
t. 416 987 8000
f. 416 987 8001
e. melina.zeppieri@gmail.com
www.melinazeppieri.com

LINKEDIN -   www.linkedin.com/in/melinazeppieri
FACEBOOK -   www.facebook.com/melina.zeppieri
TWITTER -   www.twitter.com/melinazeppieri
INSTAGRAM -   www.instagram.com/melina.zeppieri

CERTIFICATIONS:

ONTARIO COLLEGE OF TEACHERS OCT # 374557
REAL ESTATE COUNCIL OF ONTARIO [RECO]REG. # 4782000
MEMBER IN GOOD STANDING:
MEMBER OF CANADIAN REAL ESTATE ASSOCIATION [CREA]
MEMBER OF ONTARIO REAL ESTATE ASSOCIATION[OREA]
MEMBER OF TORONTO REGIONAL REAL ESTATE BOARD[TRREB]

DESIGNATIONS:

MASTER CERTIFIED NEGOTIATION EXPERT [MCNE]@
ACCREDITED SENIORS AGENT [ASA] @PIVOTAL
ACCREDITED BUYERS REPRESENTATIVE [ABR]@
LUXURY LISTING SPECIALIST [LUXE]@

Notes: ✍

SALARY PLUS PASSIVE INCOME
Zenobia Omarali

I started out my career as an educator, but I wanted to branch out into investing in order to realize true financial security that would last a lifetime and provide for my family. Education is the key to success, a theme threaded throughout my life. Knowing that I was responsible for managing my own future felt like a daunting task, so from a young age I focused and studied. I earned my degree in computer science with a minor in business.

Fortunately, my university program included a co-operative education component that gave me the opportunity to have work experience in the industry. By the time I graduated, I already had experience working for Bell-Northern Research/Nortel, the Ontario government, Facelle Royale Company and as a teacher's assistant when I was at University. Co-operative education was helpful for me to understand the importance of academic relevance to the workplace, I highly recommend it! I loved learning so much that I continued my education to complete a master's degree in system design engineering.

Being an Employee: Safe & Low Risk

Reality set in when it was time for me to work full-time. Before I knew it, I became an *"employee."* I worked in the technology field which gave me an enormous amount of satisfaction, but between traveling and major projects, it did not leave time for family. The industry was essentially a man's world.

I reflected on how my mother, who was an elementary school teacher, was able to be with our family during the week, on the weekend and spent holidays with us. She made herself available to us and that is what I wanted for my family! I also wanted to do what I loved. I always liked helping others and I had multiple teaching assistant positions which made me realize my passion. I gained great satisfaction from helping others as I shared my expertise. This made me change direction to become a high school teacher. I earned my degree in education, and I was fortunate enough to be hired as a computer science teacher.

In education, gender-based pay equity is the norm and your track record is an open book. I took advantage of opportunities at the Toronto Board of Education and I was later hired as a Department Head, then an Instructional Leader and later, to be the District-Wide Coordinator in business studies. I enjoyed being an educator because I was able to make an impact on the next generation both academically and by creating volunteer opportunities for students in both the school and the community.

I firmly believe in educating students about financial literacy. All Business Studies teachers in our schools must teach the overall and specific expectations set by the provincial government, unfortunately, the Ontario government has no Business Studies course dedicated to financial literacy and the curriculum has not been updated by the government since 2006, over 15 years ago! There is a gap between the government business curriculum and everyday real-world financial demands. I can only hope a Business Studies based financial literacy course will be introduced by the Ontario government in the near future to fill the gap.

As a teacher in Ontario, I had a sound salary, health, dental, sick leave benefits, and pension, however, I was earning a fixed amount and I was in a high tax bracket both federally and provincially, and I was still just an *"employee."*

Becoming an Investor: Investing in Real Estate & Generating Passive Income

Boxed in! With a fixed income and paying high-income taxes, I felt boxed in and I needed an out! I liked the stability and security of being an educator, but I wanted to increase my cash flow by adding passive income. With this in mind, I investigated the real estate field and purchased my first property to rent out.

I realized there was a lot of profit to be made in flipping a house, however, that would mean that I would need to have reliable and trustworthy tradespeople to do repairs/renovations on everything from plumbing and carpentry, to painting and electrical work. I did not have the contacts, nor did I have the time to dedicate to renovating a house, or the financial resources to qualify for a mortgage without a tenant. I knew the limitations of my expertise.

I decided to purchase a Toronto condo in a desirable location accessible to the TTC, enhanced with luxury features including tennis courts, workout, and meeting rooms. My first purchase was a one-bedroom plus den condominium with parking with an awesome view of Toronto's skyline. It was easy to rent, and it attracted tenants with established careers who were able to supply the necessary background information for the real estate agent.

Success! After paying monthly expenses, condo fees and taxes I had money left over, positive passive cash flow! However, this strategy required a significant down payment upon closing, and it takes years to save that amount of money.

Toronto's condo market is growing, it's the largest city in Canada and it not only serves as a hub for numerous business and sports/entertainment venues, but its multicultural welcoming nature attracts a range of people including new immigrants and Canadians wanting to live in a big city. I also did not want to be an absentee landlord, I wanted to live and work in the same city where I owned my property.

My strategy was to purchase property at today's prices that allowed me time to pay the down payment in the future – by purchasing a condo before the builder broke ground! I purchased condos at pre-construction prices where the builder required staggered down payments often in 5% increments for the next couple years. That gave me time to accumulate a significant down payment, and then qualify for a mortgage when the condominium was completed.

A one bedroom plus den worked best for me as the rent was reasonable and a couple could comfortably live in that amount of space. And, with two incomes, they could easily afford the rent. Something to consider when purchasing a unit is that the higher the floor, the higher the cost of the condo. Personally, my strategy was to purchase a one bedroom on a lower floor (to keep the cost of the unit down) in a convenient downtown location. Remember location, location, location!

Dealing with tenants has its ups and downs. High-end condos naturally attract higher salary individuals with a steady income who often stay for years. In the beginning, I used to vet the tenants myself but due to time constraints I now use qualified real estate agents to interview and assess the tenant. I manage the unit myself, providing lease renewals and the annual rent increase paperwork. In Ontario, the Landlord and Tenant Board sets out the allowable rent increase annually. Remember to increase the rent as property taxes and condo fees increase each year.

A good practice to get into is to improve the unit between each tenant. This could take the form of replacing doors, painting or be as extensive as updating kitchen appliances/cabinetry or the bathroom. In this way you can keep your condo up-to-date and looking trendy.

Keep Up on Repairs & Renovations to Protect Your Investment

Maintaining your unit not only keeps your tenants happy but it also keeps your unit up-to-date and adds value to your condo. The key is getting someone reliable to do the repairs if you can't do it yourself. I had someone in my community who represented himself as trustworthy and reliable, however, he had the gift of the gab, but he was essentially a wolf in sheep's clothing, promising to do the repairs by getting someone else to fix the problem and then mysteriously losing the invoice and overcharging for a repair.

Don't fall into that trap! Always have a written agreement, text, or email, prior to the repair and then pay by e-transfer or cheque with the person's name on it as proof of payment since repairs are tax deductible against the income of your property. Always use a reputable firm/person for repairs, even if it costs a little more, and get an invoice.

It may surprise you, but your condo building often has preferred trades workers or companies who are familiar with the building to do repairs on the building, so ask your condo management office for a recommendation. Remember to keep the invoices for the upgrades, not only for income tax but it adds to the capital cost you put into your unit for resale. (Remember, "Capital cost" equals the amount paid for the unit plus upgrades/renovations).

Be Aware of the "Sharing Economy": Lessons Learned from Airbnb Nightmares

Disruptors exist in every industry, and Airbnb, a company that is part of the "sharing economy," is a significant disruptor in the rental industry. In my property portfolio, I had a jewel of a property, a luxury two-level loft in the heart of downtown Toronto. One day I surprisingly stumbled upon my loft being illegally advertised on Airbnb for $150 per night by my tenant! Considering my tenant was paying only $1,700 per month; the tenant was making more money by subletting my loft on Airbnb in two weeks than they paid me for one month's rent. I paid the condo fees and all utilities, and they were illegally profiting by making over $3,000 tax free dollars per month by subletting my loft on Airbnb.

This was not my biggest concern. The compelling issue was my condo insurance clearly stated that my coverage was nullified if the unit was used for short term rental! In addition, short term rentals were clearly against Tridel Property Management's condo rules. No property insurance! That meant that if there was any property damage to my loft or a flood in the condo unit, my insurance would not cover the expense, and I would be out of pocket for thousands of dollars.

I confronted the tenant, and they claimed ignorance of the rules and restrictions. Illegally renting out property without permission is never acceptable. When I contacted Airbnb, they made light of the issue and simply e-mailed a generic form response. The tenant signed a cease and desist agreement but did not comply and one of the Airbnb guests e-mailed me a complaint!

When I consulted my lawyer, he stated that I would not be able to evict my tenant because I could not prove my property was currently being listed on Airbnb! The past sublet violation would not be recognized. Currently, there are no city rules/by-laws that exist in Toronto, nor are there any clauses in the Landlord and Tenant Act that I could use to evict the tenant based on the illegal Airbnb sublet.

To make a long story short, I was eventually able to evict him based on an Ontario Fire Code violation. The tenant had an open flame gas heater on the patio which violated the City Fire Code. They were given a written order to remove the heater by the Property Manager but did not comply. The good news is that the Landlord and Tenant Board evicted that tenant from my loft, but the bad news is that they still owe me rent.

The Airbnb issue is still not resolved in Toronto. Ideally, West Hollywood, California has it right! Their City Hall voted to ban renters from making money from short-term Airbnb stays. The City only allows home and condominium owners to rent out a portion of their residence for short stays, and more importantly, it makes it illegal for renters to sublet.

Chicago, Illinois also has strict guidelines. It has firm Airbnb criteria including a $500 application, home ownership, liability insurance, taxes on the gross income and City inspection and certification of the unit! Unfortunately, the Airbnb has launched a legal appeal in the Ontario courts against Toronto's proposed Airbnb rules so there is still not a definitive law restricting the use of short-term rentals.

Don't Underestimate the Power of Insurance: Liability & Protection

Insurance is vital! Make sure you have extensive *Property Insurance* coverage on your rental unit. I have dealt with a variety of bumps on the road including flood damage in the condo that extended to the unit below and an alleged dog bite accusation. Fortunately, my insurance covered everything.

Also, make sure your tenant has *Renter's Insurance*. The tenant's policy should cover their personal property and if the tenant has a dog/pet, it should cover the pet's liability. I always include a conditional clause in the rental agreement to ensure that the tenant has their own rental insurance.

Taking preventive action to ensure your property stays in your name is also a priority of mine! I have always purchased *Title Insurance*, to make sure my name is securely attached to my property. Having it gives you peace of mind that your property is protected against potential fraudsters who may try to take out a mortgage on your property.

The final insurance I advise you to take is *Life Insurance*. Having a positive cash flow is of great comfort, but if something happens to you, the rent may not cover all the expenses that your loved ones may encounter. Everything from inheritance tax, land transfer tax to funeral expenses can be covered with the proceeds of your life insurance which is always tax free.

My advice is to purchase life insurance from an insurance agency, not a bank. I have found that banks have too many conditions and outs like hidden clauses including voiding coverage due to pre-existing conditions and other restrictions. I found that established life insurance agencies do a thorough job of assessing you before issuing the policy. Universal life insurance worked with me because it includes an investment portion, but you can also look into whole, term, or permanent insurance.

I was fortunate enough to meet Que Yazdani, an insurance and financial expert from the World Financial Group who helped me with my decision. He also introduced me to a way that I could make my own referral fees when I purchased life insurance, property mortgages from banks or secondary lenders, automobile insurance, and even when I made investments.

Que holds financial literacy courses in his Richmond Hill office which were very insightful. I liked the education resources so much that I also decided to study for the Life License Qualification Program (LLQP) and earned my mutual fund license. Now I have a licence in both and if I have to pay commission on insurance, mortgage or mutual funds transactions, the money goes to me!

Know Your Personal Risk Tolerance

Today I have passive income as an *investor* and the career that I always wanted, being an educator. I'm an *"employee"* by choice. Being an educator gives me quality time with my family while managing my passive investments. As a female visible minority, I wanted to have the security that in the future I would have a variety of passive income when I retire including rental income and dividend investments, plus a teacher's pension, allowing me to make ends meet while I pursue other passions.

Sharing my story and my lessons learned is important to me. Personally, I have a low risk tolerance. I wanted the security of a steady income and the benefits of passive income.

My journey led me to be a teacher, an educational leader and a volunteer coordinator facilitating at the school and community level. Today, I'm a guidance counsellor, a position I've always wanted ever since I saw the old television show "Room 222" when I was a child. I turned to real estate to generate my passive income. Your risk tolerance may be higher, perhaps you can go full time in the real estate rental market, but I know I can only cope with a little volatility. Knowing what makes you happy is very important in life and then the next step is to make it happen!

Cultivate a "Can Do" Mindset

If I can help empower others to succeed and become more financially stable, then I would have reached my goal. I have included a condo purchase/lease content checklist and key definitions I have found to be top considerations when purchasing a rental unit. If you don't have a lot of time or expertise to dedicate to flipping a house, I suggest buying a condominium.

If you don't have enough for a down payment, I would suggest creating a joint venture with a family member or friend. The *Stress Test* in Canada (a financial test that calculates how much property you can afford to mortgage) is quite rigid so you may have to get allies in order to purchase your property. Remember, trust in God, but tie your camel. If you do a joint venture, make sure you get a lawyer and document your agreement. If you don't like the high prices in the Toronto real estate market, look elsewhere. I suggest a University town where the real estate entry point is lower.

Whatever you do, remove the word "don't" from your vocabulary and replace it with a "can do" mental mindset! Even if you have a low risk tolerance, expand yourself out of the *"employee"* box and become an *investor* with passive income!

BASIC PROPERTY INFORMATION
Property Market Value
Property Tax Assessed Value
Description: Size, Bedrooms
Door: *Number of Units generating Income*

Property Tax/year
Educational Tax Designation: *Public or Catholic Board*
Mortgage: Bank & Payment/month
Condominium Management Company & Payment/month
Utilities Supplier & Payment/month
Property Insurance: Company & Payment/month
Title Insurance & onetime payment
Life Insurance: Company & Payment/month

RENTAL INFORMATION
Property Location
Tenant Name(s)
Contact Information
Date of Lease & items to include ☐ Utilities, Parking, Lawn care ☐ Tenant Insurance: Personal Property & Pet Restriction/Conditions on: ☐ Short-term Rental (e.g. no Airbnb) ☐ Smoking/Growing Marijuana ☐ Pets (e.g. dog bite)
Rent Increase Date (12 months after signing)
Tenant Emergency Contact

Keywords/Agencies

Bank Lender: Traditional lenders refer to banks and credit unions that serve customers with good credit scores and a reliable income. There are six major banks in Canada, including Bank of Montreal or TD Bank.

"B" Lender: These institutions offer a lower barrier of entry to qualifying for a mortgage but can offset that with higher interest rates. For example, people who do not qualify for a traditional bank loan under Canada's Stress Tests or have declared bankruptcy may have to use a "B" lender such as B2B Bank.

Doors: A money generating rental unit. For example, a "four plex" is one building, but you will have four money generating units, referring to the "four" doors.

Education taxes: You must pay educational tax. In the majority of cases, it's the landlord that must pay the property and education tax. It is important to verify which school board your Education Tax is designated to fund. In Ontario, you can designate your Educational Tax to either the Public or the Catholic Board. If you are purchasing a new condo, the designated education tax can be hidden in the multi-page document, so verify where your education taxes go in order to be sure you fund your preferred educational board.

Ghost Hotels/Condos: A condo building that the majority of units are listed on short-term rentals. These types of condos can be problematic due to the transient nature of the tenants occupying the building. Check with the condo board/condo property manager about their policy on short term rentals.

Landlord and Tenant Board: The *Residential Tenancy Act* gives residential landlords and tenants rights and responsibilities, and sets out a process for enforcing them. It resolves disputes between landlords and tenants in

Ontario through mediation or adjudication, resolves eviction applications and provides information to landlords and tenants about their rights and responsibilities under the *RTA.*

Lease/Residential Tenancy Agreement: A *Standard Form of Lease* - Form 047-2229E is **required** for private **residential** tenancies for new agreements signed on or after April 30, 2018 in Ontario as enacted by the Ontario Ministry of Municipal Affairs and Housing. The *Standard Form of Lease* is available in many languages from Arabic to Vietnamese so the tenant can gain a sound interpretation of the Lease in Ontario's multilingual/multicultural society.

Recommended Addendums to the Lease Agreement can be made as an Appendix listing additional terms in section 15 of the lease. I recommend including:

- ☐ Short-term rental restrictions (e.g., Airbnb)

- ☐ No smoking, or growing marijuana

- ☐ Tenant must have their own Property & Pet insurance

- ☐ Pet information and liability

- ☐ Utilities clarification

Rent Increase/Rent Control: The landlord can only increase the rent once every 12 months and must give the tenant 90 days written notice. The increase is calculated using the Provincial Consumer Price Index. In Ontario use a *N1 Form Notice of Rent Increase* (2.2% in 2020) or in British Columbia use the *RTO7 Form* for a 2.6% rent increase.

Sharing Economy & Airbnb: Assets or services are shared between private individuals, for a fee, typically ordered/paid using the Internet is the basis of the sharing economy. Airbnb, Inc. is an online marketplace used to arrange lodging. The company does not own any of the real estate listings, it acts as a broker, receiving commissions from each booking. It is such a new way of generating money that cities/governments have yet to implement rules and regulations to govern who can rent units, or who is responsible for liabilities or taxes.

Stress Test/Mortgage Qualifying Tool: This calculator is set by the Government of Canada. The Financial Consumer Agency determines whether or not you can qualify for a home mortgage based on income and expenses. The Mortgage Qualifying Tool typically uses a median five-year fixed insured mortgage rate from mortgage insurance applications, plus 2%.

Recommended Books

Rich Dad Poor Dad
Warner Books Ed, Robert Kiyosaki, ISBN-13: 978-1365076350

Saving Your Future: Basic Principles of Building a Financial Foundation
World System Builder, ISBN-13: 978-1936914050

Financial Foundation Educational Program Workbook
Mass Market Paperback, Xuan Nguyen, ISBN-13: 978-1936914128

ABOUT THE AUTHOR

Zenobia Omarali is an educator, entrepreneur, real estate investor and coach. She believes education is a great equalizer and should be accessible to all. Moreover, understanding financial education and strategies is very important to secure a sound foundation for life and creating comfort so one can have the luxury of spending more time with family and helping others. Sharing lessons learned from her experiences, academic research, and studying trends is important to her so she can help others gain insight into financial strategies.

As a real estate investor, Zenobia has had various experiences with finance, tenants, and maintenance issues that she can share to benefit others who want to invest in real estate. Using real estate to generate long term passive income to generate supplemental income and finance life into retirement is one of her strategies. Her chosen career is an educator which gives her joy and supports her real estate investment. Making money work for you instead of just working for money is a key concept to life. In addition to real estate investment, she is also certified as an Insurance and a Mutual Fund Agent because if there was a commission to be paid, she would earn the referral fee, surcharge or premium herself rather than paying someone else.

As an educator for over twenty-five years, she has had various leadership roles from Business Department Head to District-Wide Co-ordinator in Business at the Toronto District School

Board. She has lead curriculum writing teams to help engage students in financial education by creating various course resources from developing an interdisciplinary high school course, Financial Securities, to course supplements for Introduction to Business and more. Her background in the field of Business, Computer Science, and a Masters Degree in System Design Engineering from the University of Waterloo has served her well as an observer and systems thinker.

Zenobia believes in helping others and leaving a positive imprint creates good karma. In addition, by sharing her experiences, she is able to help create success for others. She is a mother, wife, sister, daughter, investor, coach, and educator. A special gratitude goes to her parents, who had the foresight to leave a life of comfort and immigrate to Canada to create a new beginning in the land of opportunity and potential.

E-mail: zenomarali@gmail.com
LinkedIn: Zenobia S. Omarali
Website: zenobiaomarali/weebly.com
Office: 1 West Pearce St, Suite 705, Richmond Hill, ON L4B 3K3
Mentor: Que Yazdani, World Financial Group

Notes:

A PARTNER IN CREATING BUSINESS SUCCESS
Mayur Gandhi, CPA, CA

Mayur Gandhi is an accomplished Chartered Professional Accountant (CPA). He is a partner at G + G Partners LLP, Chartered Professional Accountants in Toronto, Canada. He has many titles including father, husband, business owner and leader. He is driven and ambitious in everything he does and he cares deeply about people and especially his clients. As a trusted advisor, Mayur takes his role very seriously by up-leveling his knowledge continuously so that his clients are educated and protected. Moreover, his knowledge and expertise in the area of small and medium sized businesses is outstanding.

Turning ideas and dreams into a business

A new business owner or an individual who has never been self-employed may have a lot of questions before taking the leap. Their concerns are often related to job security, losing a regular salary, and figuring out how to structure their new venture. Once the client is ready to start working on turning their idea into a business, my firm guides them on how to create a strategy to move forward. New business owners must ensure all registrations are done on time and in a proper manner. This is the backbone of a successful business.

A good foundation is laid well before new business owners start their venture. Consulting with my firm before making any decisions creates effective and efficient results.

Incorporating or operating as a sole proprietor, partnership or corporate structure, are some of the early selections that help shape the future of the business.

At some point the agreement to move forward and turn an idea into a real business is financial. There is always a need for capital.

A new business owner may need money for:

- Setting up an office space

- Promoting the new venture through advertising

- Meeting with potential clients

- Developing prototypes

- Doing (market) research

These are some initial expenditures that may incur, even before any revenue is generated.

At the beginning, we work closely to educate the client about the necessary tax compliance requirements. We go over the timeline for the year and make sure clients are punctual with those. Business owners not only have the obligation to complete income tax filings, but also to be compliant with other filing requirements including and not limited to sales tax (GST/HST) as well as payroll. These have to be filed and paid on time or the business could face penalties and interest charges.

As business continues, clients need advice on many issues on an on-going basis. For example, should they buy or lease a vehicle? Buying or leasing a new space? This type of advice goes beyond the functions performed by accountants. At my firm, we offer such consulting services to our clients as and when need arises in their business.

Understanding the process of consulting with a CPA

During the first meeting with a business owner, we seek to understand our client's business. Having taken our time to do so, the next step is to gather all the necessary information to prepare the filings that may be required. Sometimes clients do not know what is needed; so we work closely with them to emphasize the need for the necessary documentation. This could mean going back a number of years for unfiled returns.

I am an accountant, consultant and an advisor to my clients and my role is to educate them on each step of the accounting process. This way, clients are on the same page as us which fosters collaboration and partnership. When they realize what is needed, and why it is needed, the process becomes smooth and we can produce the results the client is looking for. I am pleased to say that my clients appreciate my efficient and collaborative approach.

Keeping good documentation is as important as generating sales and profits.

Navigating the Toronto real estate market

The Toronto real estate market has been on the rise for the last number of years as it has seen an influx of money and investment. Meeting with clients who are investing in real estate involves consultations on the structure of ownership, and the related tax implications.

Some questions clients often ask are:

- How to own and hold a real estate portfolio?

- Is it to be purchased and owned personally, in a trust, partnership or corporation?

- What expenses are deductible from the investment income the property generates?

- How to address GST/HST implications?

Self-employed corporate business owners have certain flexibility to do income and tax planning. With prices rising in the Greater Toronto Area, clients often think about refinancing and using some of their existing equity to invest further. These transactions also have certain tax implications the client needs to know about.

There are clients who have never owned a home and want to be homeowners. First time homebuyers have certain tax credits available to them. There is the *Canada First Time Homebuyer Incentive* that can help in the purchase of a first home. In this program, it contributes a down-payment of 5% or 10% of the purchase price. There is also the *Homebuyer Plan* that allows the withdrawal of funds from an RRSP (up to the allowed limits) with no tax withholdings. There are qualifying criteria for these plans that the client must meet.

There are many advantages to speaking to an accountant before choosing to buy real estate. Each client's situation is unique. My job is to assess and advise based on their individual requirements.

Frequently asked questions relating to first time home buyers

- Is there any assistance from the government that we can receive towards the down payment of our home? Do we qualify for the Canada first time homebuyer's incentive?

- Do we qualify for the homebuyer's plan?

- How can we develop room for RRSP to achieve our target of withdrawal under the homebuyer's plan?

- Are there any other tax rebates that are available to first-time homebuyers once we close on a property?

My story

I arrived from New Delhi, India to Canada at the age of nineteen having never lived away from home and family. The transition as a first year undergrad was difficult, and I struggled with homesickness in ways I had never experienced before. Nevertheless, my journey of coming to Canada taught me many lessons such as learning to cook for myself, meeting new people, and the ability to focus on my studies. Although this time was challenging and new, it was life changing!

While studying at University, I had to make a choice between different streams under the business program; I chose accounting. The accounting courses proved to be both intriguing and interesting to me. The more I learned, the more I wanted to learn.

Upon graduating, I moved to Calgary and started articling with an accounting firm where I worked for a few years and completed my Chartered Accounting designation. I worked mainly with small to medium sized businesses as well as not-for-profit organisations, Aboriginal communities and First Nations.

My experiences working in Calgary got me excited about the field of public accounting, working directly with clients and servicing the needs of owner-managed businesses. Then I moved from Calgary back to Toronto where I began working for another accounting firm prior to starting my own.

Perseverance and a positive attitude takes you a long way...

It has been a long journey for me to come this far. I am a strong believer in planning and preparing for the long term. This is the advice my parents gave me while growing up, and what I share with my clients on a day to day basis as well.

Focusing on growth and having a long term vision has always been a signature quality for me. This attitude and resilient mindset have helped me to become the man I am today, both personally and professionally. It has served me in the roles I play as a son, husband, brother, and father.

Challenges have also made me a strong person. I am proud to have my own wonderful set of clients whom I see as my family.

Working with great minds

In the world of accounting, we come across a lot of professionals from other fields. We speak to bankers for financing requirements and applications for our clients. Clients look to us to help them achieve all the documentation the bank requests to finance their business or investment needs. As an advisor, we equip clients with the knowledge of what the bank requires.

Lawyers are another group of professionals we work with quite extensively because they are involved in the legal process with the bankers or mortgage brokers. If a client is buying or selling real-estate or a business, there are legal requirements to adhere to. If they want to rent a space, a lawyer may help them understand the contract and the legal obligations. We do not go into the legal space of the contract. My role is to assist my clients to understand the financial aspects and obligations they are agreeing to and help business owners create their budgets. For example, we might point out potential cash flow issues that the client might face because of the new contract.

We also represent our clients with CRA enquiries and audits. Sometimes CRA audits clients regarding their filings including income taxes, GST/HST filings and payroll remittances. Speaking to a CRA representative and preparing for CRA audits can be stressful. The key is to have all necessary documentation in place and we assist our clients through the entire process.

An accountant's advice

As a professional accountant servicing the business community in Toronto and surrounding areas, we deal with a plethora of clients across a variety of industries. We understand numbers and the fun of doing business.

As an entrepreneur, clients take the risk by giving up secure employment, not getting a steady paycheque, employing people and taking on debt. When the client requires advice along this stressful and powerful journey, my firm is right here to guide them, support them and help them. We simply ask clients to speak with us before, and not after the fact. It is better to know options ahead of time because this creates a strong foundation for a sustainable business partnership and helps save time and money.

I am here to address your unique accounting needs. The best way to contact me is:

PHONE: 416.222.2780
EMAIL: mayur@mgcpaca.ca

ABOUT THE AUTHOR

Mayur Gandhi is passionate about people, work and his clients. A Chartered Professional Accountant (CPA) by profession, he takes pride in being a trusted advisor to his clients, supporting their accounting needs, and providing tax compliance and assurance services. Mayur's education spans across two continents. Having spent his school life in India, he completed his Bachelors in Business Administration (BBA) at the University of Toronto and then proceeded to obtain his CPA, CA designation. He has worked extensively with public accounting firms in Calgary and Toronto in personal and corporate tax, assurance, accounting and management consulting. He now has a practice of his own in Toronto, which serves clients across various industries. A visionary by nature, Mayur is always on the lookout for new opportunities to grow. Focus, planning and a positive attitude have helped shape his professional journey. Besides his work, he has a keen interest in travelling, sports, and cars. A game of golf, and a great meal with family and friends helps him unwind over the weekends. He is happily married to his wife Arpita, and they are blessed with a 2-year-old son Atharv, who has added a new dimension to their lives.

GLOSSARY

CPA: CHARTERED PROFESSIONAL ACCOUNTANT
CRA: CANADA REVENUE AGENCY
GST: GOODS AND SERVICES TAX
HST: HARMONIZED SALES TAX
GTA: GREATER TORONTO AREA
RRSP: REGISTERED RETIREMENT SAVINGS PLAN

Notes:

Notes: ✍

RULE LIKE A QUEEN &
CONQUER CLIENT ATTRACTION
WITH GRACE AND EASE

Fatima Omar Khamissa

The perfect prospect to work with us is a woman who has life-experience, past skills and wants to use her history to make a difference for other women.

She wants time-freedom.

She comes from the corporate world and she has worked very, very hard. She has a lot of experience and she is not being appreciated. She is between forty and fifty years old. She has decided that she wants to build her own coaching business. She wants to break the glass-ceiling so she can create a business that she absolutely loves.

She loves making a difference for other people. She's ready to take her skills, her expertise, and turn it into a purpose.

You might be asking, "Why would she want to achieve this outcome?"

If she's been in the corporate world and she is already making six figures, she realizes that she is not actually getting paid for her expertise. She has been shortchanged. Working for someone else is amazing and there's a lot of reward, but her creativity has been stifled. When she launches herself as a coach, she can take everything she's gone through in her life – her work, her skills, her expertise, her knowledge, her experiences, and support other women and *she can charge exactly what she's worth*.

At the Million Stars Academy Certification Program, we equip and support women over 40 to step into their brilliance so she can transform her past experiences into purpose, power and profit. We equip her with step-by-step guide, templates, and everything she needs to launch and build a successful coaching business and get clients even before she is certified.

In the second stage of her life, she's able to create an amazing income working on her time and changing the lives of women everywhere.

People often ask me how I got into this business.

What led me into this field is experiencing a violent, abusive relationship. I was married to a man who was diagnosed with bipolar narcissistic disorder, and after twenty one years, and eleven months, I took my five kids and I left. I wasn't able to work or have friends. Everything was designed to keep me isolated. I had no work-experience, and I had five children with this man, which (side note) are the complete blessings and the gemstones and the absolute gold in my life.

So, when I left with the five kids, I was terrified. I had never ever been officially employed. I was a homeschool mom. All the social activities in the community took place at my home. My husband was going to bring home the deer, and he failed at that as well.

So I waited for both my parents to die, and then I left.

I didn't know how to make money. My creativity and my confidence was completely broken and stumped, and the horrors of my painful past kept me in a loop of nightmares.

I desperately wanted to help other women. I knew I could talk about my experience. I wanted to talk to my younger self and tell her about my life as a battered wife and educate her about the signs of violence.

So, that's what I did. I started speaking publically, volunteering at jails and immigration Centre's, speaking for free, and sharing my painful past. A documentary was made about my life that won first prize at a local film festival. I kept putting myself out there and sharing my story to benefit other women and to give them hope.

I applied for many jobs. They were going to pay me $16 an hour and I needed a professional personal support worker to take care of my son Tarik. Tarik has cerebral palsy and scoliosis. These professionals charge at least $20.00 an hour to look after my son who cannot go to the bathroom on his own. It just wasn't going to work for me. The math didn't make any sense.

Somewhere along the line, I realized, there must be a business I could create. I can make a little bit of money. I can work part-time on my business, have my children with me, and still take care for my disabled son, Tarik.

That's how I got into the business.

I quickly learned that there was real power in what I was tapping into. I got to see for myself firsthand what it was like to do what I did – change the lives of other people and make money to support my family. This became my passion. I still wake up every single day excited to see whose life I'm going to change.

Let's talk about obstacles, misconceptions and pitfalls. If you're reading this right now and you're curiously thinking, "I want to be a coach. I really want to do this and it's something that a lot of people are doing. I see coaches online all the time making money and changing lives."

The first thing you want to do is *fix your mindset*. If you say, "I want to be a coach", and you don't realize what you're getting yourself into, the business, the strategy and the immense hard work. You will set yourself up for heartbreak, blame and failure.

It takes time to build a great business. Nothing happens overnight. Go in with your eyes wide open.

Here are 7 tips to get started:

- Number one - it's going to cost money. This is not a job where you go into work, you get trained, you get a little uniform, and then they pay you for showing up. No, this is your own baby. You're going to put your money where your mouth is. You're going to have to step it up. You're going to have to go through modules. You're going to have to go through self-directed learning. And you're going to have to do create massive implementation. So get your mindset right.

- Number two - schedule everything. Remember when you were in school, and the teacher took attendance to make sure everyone was in class – in your own business, ***no one's going to take attendance***. No one's going to ask you if you've done your work. You probably already have a job. This may be your side gig. You should schedule everything. You fill in your calendar and the calendar runs you. No mommy or teacher or professor is going to come and smack your hand or reprimand you if you don't do it. If you don't do it, you don't do it. So, you have to be your own policeman. You want to schedule everything in your calendar, I mean everything. Spending time with your children, calendar it. Your weekly massage, calendar it. Having a meditation session, calendar it. Everything has to be on the calendar.

- Number three - Be flexible with your calendar. That's part of the business of working for yourself. Bring playfulness and fun to your life. Keep your promises to yourself and have enjoyment. You want to be flexible with your calendar

- Number four - Self-care. Take good care of yourself. Your mind, your body, your spirit. Affirmations, exercise, good food, prayer and rest. Remind yourself of how wonderful you are, how awesome you are, and all the things that you're going to accomplish. Tell yourself:

  - *I am a million dollar coach.*
  - *I am a magnet for clients.*
  - *People love what I do.*
  - *My clients are so amazing.*
  - *They get amazing, fantastic, incredible results.*
  - *I get the best testimonials.*
  - *My website rocks because I'm a rock star coach.*

Say these over and over again.

- Number five - Belief. You must believe that you are going to get this thing done. You have to believe you're actually going to achieve your dreams. No kidding. A declaration and a belief that you are 100% going to achieve it. What I mean by this is you see it. You feel it. You act it. In the morning before you get out of bed, lay there for an extra five minutes and visualize who you are becoming. A rock star coach. A million dollar coach. A global coach. Every part of you has to believe that this is already a done deal and it's on its way towards you.

- Number six – Gratefulness. Gratefulness is the secret ingredient for abundance. When I was collecting welfare, I didn't have enough money buy chicken for my children. Bread and beans were our staple diet. There were many aspects of my life that were sad and miserable. I knew if I focused on the negative stuff, I would get more to be resentful for. So I focused on what was working. I focused on the good stuff. I would take my journal and write what I saw in my room:

  - *I am grateful for the chair I am sitting in.*
  - *I am grateful for the refrigerator, the stove and the toaster.*
  - *I am grateful for my eyes and the legs that can walk to the kitchen.*
  - *I am grateful for the ability to lock my door and be safe.*
  - *I am grateful that my children are with me.*

  Focus on what you have, and you will
  have more to be grateful for.

- Number seven - Be willing to unlearn. If you knew how to do build a successful coaching business, you would have already done it. Don't you agree? So, you got to be willing to say, "I'm going to take all my current knowledge and put it inside in a little compartment. I'm going to pretend like I don't know. I'm going to trust my mentor. I'm going to trust my coach. I'm going to follow what they say as long as it's not illegal". Because everything you already know is in your history. If you keep doing what you have done, you will keep getting what you got. To create something new and different is outside of your comfort zone and it's going to get very uncomfortable. Guess what? *All your success lies outside your comfort zone*. Be willing to unlearn what doesn't work and learn what works.

Red Emerald Mentoring & Training is Fatima's High-End One-On-One Personal Program.
She Only Takes On Six Women Per Year In This Highly Specialized Program.

Now let's move to the solution. How do you avoid and overcome some of the obstacles in your journey to become a rock star coach? At the Million Stars Academy Coaching Certification Program, we have mindset calls every single week. Because what I've learned is that *it doesn't matter how much I tell you what to do, your inner conversation will dictate your results*.

Take Michelle, who wants to lose weight. She is very, very clear about the how. She has been given a healthy food-guide to follow. She bought a gym membership. The doctor told her to eat less and move more. So why is she not losing weight and has not changed her eating habits?

Take Joanne, who has $50,000 of student debt. Her financial planner tells her to make more money and spend less. But she doesn't believe that this is possible.

Take Melanie, who signed up for Million Stars Academy. Her dream was to become a successful coach to help other women. When it's time to do her modules, she makes excuses. She watches television or cleans the bathroom.

What do these three women have in common?

Negative self-talk. What they say to themselves when no-one is listening. It's all in the mind. We know this. It's the human condition. We can tell somebody, "Do X, Y, Z,", and they don't.

There's nothing wrong with you. Everyone does it. It's the human condition.

And for that reason, we have a mindset calls to help you to get through those negative thoughts. We also give you all the step-by-step guides, and templates. So you don't have to reinvent the wheel.

We've done it. We've tried it. We have failed. We have fallen. We've gotten up and we know what works. So everything we are sharing with you works.

Simply follow the templates and the step-by-step guides.

We help you to fail less, to get success right away because we want you to get clients while you are being certified.

All you have to do is show up and take action. Show up on the call, listen to the modules, and implement. That's all you have to do. You don't have to think about all the stuff. Everything is already given to you.

A lot of people ask me, "Was I always like this? What did I change in my thinking? Did I change it or was I always like this? What about my beliefs?"

I don't want to repeat the things that I have written in my other books, I'm not that kind of author.

In a nutshell, I grew up being a very nice girl. A good girl. I was the good daughter that always listened to my parents. I always thought that my happiness and my success were other people's happiness and other people's success. So if my father was happy, I was happy. If my husband was successful, I was successful. I didn't know anything about me or my dreams.

If you had asked me, "What will make you happy or what are your dreams?" I had no idea how to answer the question.

From that good obedient girl to travel this journey and arrive here, it took me years and years of unlearning.

Unlearning how to people-please.

Unlearning how to listen and obey.

Unlearning being fearful of others.

Unlearning everything that wasn't working.

We might think we are living in this world but the truth is we are not.

> **We are living in our minds**. Your success depends on how big your mind is and what you believe about this world and what you can achieve. When you change how you think, your results will change.

How does that work?

When you change the way you think, you change your feelings. When you change your feelings, you change your behaviour. When your actions change, your results change.

Good or bad. Positive or negative. The loop remains the same.

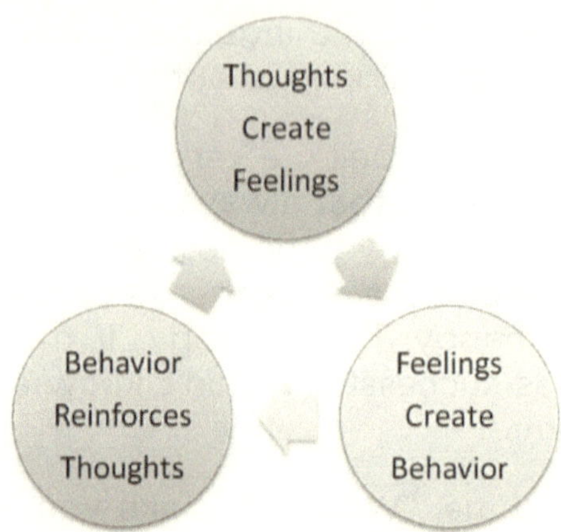

Have I ever failed?

Wow! Yes. I have failed more than any other person I know and I'm finally okay with it. I'm finally okay with failing. I'm finally okay with not simply being okay with failing, but completely falling in love with failing. My philosophy is **fail forward faster**. The faster I fail, the faster the team fails, the faster we're going to find all the ways that didn't work. Entrepreneurship is about failing.

When you join The Million Stars Academy Certification Program, you're going to fail. Trust me, you're going to fail. We're going to send you all the scripts on how to do a discovery call and you're going to fail.

The key is that you're NOT going to do one call or two calls and then fail and decide, "I'm not really good at discovery calls".

So, what did I do? I promised myself I would do a hundred discovery calls every single day, and I failed, and I failed. But guess what happened? I had a hundred names in front me and I was failing, and failing, and failing.

I was excited, "Yeah, I have more names to call. This is great practice. I could keep doing calls. I could do this all day".

If you only have three names on your desk and all three hang up on you, how are you going to feel for the rest of the day? The secret is to position yourself with so many name, you run out of time before you run out of motivations.

Falling in love with failure is really important to your success as a business owner. It's actually magical to fail because finding all the ways that don't work opens up all the possibilities for what works. Failure is also a leadership quality. It's about not taking things so seriously. When you lighten up, you don't take things so seriously, you're more successful, because you get to enjoy your success more. Your whole attitude changes.

I often think about my younger self. That, innocent, beautiful, young Fatima. I'll sometimes look at pictures of my younger self and wonder, what I would say to her as the wise, big sister, or as an elder auntie. This is what I'd say, *"Darling, lighten up a bit. Dream big, girl, dream big. Take care of your health, and rest, when needed. Don't push yourself so much, and take time with self-care and cultivate self-respect. Study hard. Love your parents. Put God first. Everything will be fine".*

Balance is a very interesting subject because I don't believe in balance. Balance is something that is a strange phenomenon. When I'm excited about a project, all my energy will be focused there. If I'm home with my kids and we're cooking for the day, then I focus all my energy on that. As long as you get stuff done in a week, you might not get the same stuff done every single day. I am not a multitasker. I focus on one thing and get it done. Then I move onto the next thing.

Let's talk about habits. Tony Robbins says that habits will help you fail, or habits will help you succeed. Habits are really important because habits dictate the results of your life, how you think, and who you become.

Have you ever been to an event where 100 people were attending? How easy is it to tell who eats well and works out regularly? It's easy. The habits we do privately will be seen publicly after a couple of years of consistency. No one sees what you do privately. But it's those habits that you do every single day consistently that are going to build your business like you've never imagined.

Some of my daily habits are:

- I do my prayers.

- I read sacred text.

- I meditate.

- I journal.

- I do my stretches.

- I walk.

- I do yoga once a week.

- I'm always dreaming and creating.

These are some of the things that are part of my habits every single day.

Now, you may be thinking, "I want to be a coach. I'm going to change my mindset. I want to become a coach because it's going to be healing for me. It's going to be cathartic for me. I'm going to be able to make a difference in the world. I'm going to be able to make money while I change people's lives. So Fatima, what kind of advice would you give me?"

The first piece of advice I could give you is shop around. Look at all the different people that are training and mentoring and doing coaching programs, everywhere, online and offline.

Second, find a mentor that has walked your path. When I first started researching who I wanted to work with. I found a lot of online coaches that were doing great things. After much research, I found the one! She was amazing. She was magnetic and incredible. She was making a lot of money. She called herself the e-zine queen. I was excited to work with her for a short while. Then, I couldn't relate to her anymore. She was a single, tall, blonde woman, never been married, no children, and her struggles were so minimal in compared to mine. There I was - welfare mom, $500 check a month, five kids, a disabled child, trying to make ends meet.

What you want is to find the mentor who you can relate to. It doesn't have to be an exact story, just relatedness. You must be able to relate to her.

I hire a new coach every year. My new coach is married. Her mom is part of her master coaches. She has a husband, no kids, but I can relate to her. It's the weirdest thing. When she speaks, I understand her language. I feel confident and secure.

Find a mentor who has walked the path. Find a mentor who you can relate to. Not everyone out there is for you. If they have suffered a bit and have overcome - that is what you're looking for.

Hire someone who has your back and is committed to your success. At Million Stars Academy we give you all the templates, the step-by-step guides, everything you need to launch that business plus mindset training. We have mindset calls every single week to help you to stay on track.

We give you the opportunity to stay the course.

We give you the opportunity to stay on track.

We give you the opportunity to fail and get up again.

So, you have a very supportive team around you keeping you on track because we believe in you. We believe in your success and we want your success.

The next step for you to find out more is to join our private Facebook Group – The Tribe of Spiritual Entrepreneurs

What's cool about this training is that it's not actually one of those trainings where you go and get pitched - absolutely not. When you sign up, you will be sent a link to a webinar. The webinar is called The 10 Biggest Mistakes Women Leaders Make That Keep Them Stuck, Struggling, and Invisible. On this webinar, I pull back the curtains on exactly what women leaders, coaches, healers, therapists do that keep them failing. You will also learn seven strategies that you can implement right away.

The training will give you an incredible amount of value and it's a huge contribution that you will be able to implement in your life and your business immediately.

If you decide you like it. You resonate with me. You really want to join the program. Then, book a call with us at SpeakWithFatima.com Either myself, or one of my master coaches will get on the call with you and we'll have a conversation to see if you make a good fit for The Million Stars Program.

The Dalai Lama said, "Women are going to rule the world". I believe in my heart of hearts that women are natural entrepreneurs. I am an advocate for women to have their own businesses, create the life that they want, and make more money than their male relatives because I truly believe that when a woman has money, the world becomes a better place. So, I welcome you to the world of Million Stars. Thank you so much for reading this chapter up to here.

Big hug, Fatima.

ABOUT THE AUTHOR

For 21 years, Fatima Omar Khamissa was a victim of an abusive marriage which destroy- ed all the hopes and dreams she had for herself.

She took her five children and left that marriage and today, Fatima is the CEO of Fatima Omar International Inc., leading provider of training, coaching and publishing for women who feel stuck, frustrated, and tired of living lives without satisfaction, meaning, and progress.

The trauma of abuse, apartheid and violence was not able to break Fatima's spirit and as an international best-selling author, Fatima is sharing her message to inspire, motivate, and lead women all over the world to continual growth in both personal and professional life.

She has written 6 books, three became bestsellers on Amazon.com. After writing her books, her annual income became her monthly income and her publishing company was born. To date, she has helped more than 37 people become bestselling authors through her publishing company.

She uses psychology and brand awareness techniques to position her clients as authorities and thought-leaders in their niche. Fatima is known for her "out-of-the-box" ideas to empower, educate and inspire audiences globally. Business owners choose Fatima, because she is not "just another coach", instead she's a real business strategist and thought leader who creates custom plans for you that details practical strategies for overcoming obstacles and unlock your greatest abilities.

Fatima Omar International Inc. is a boutique personal branding firm specializing in publishing, certified coach training and press releases to create visibility, authority and expert status for their clients

They shine the spotlight on you. Their custom packages are uniquely created for you and they guarantee best seller status so you can use your bestselling book as a business card to attract higher paying clients and global speaking gigs, to make a difference and make more money.

They equip you with transforming your past pain and skills into purpose, power, and profit through coach certification training. Fatima's step-by-step guides and templates take all the guesswork out of your entrepreneurship journey in order to attract clients while you are being certified.

A third-party testimonial from a journalist that is featured on ABC, NBC, Fox, etc. is a powerful platform to create brand awareness and to catapult you into a sphere of leadership. Press releases give you instant credibility and show the world that you are the person that they should be working with.

Join Fatima in her PRIVATE FACEBOOK GROUP today.

The Tribe of Spiritual Entrepreneurs where she offers free tips and trainings every single week.

The world needs your skills and expertise

FATIMA
Omar Khamissa
EMPOWERMENT & BUSINESS COACH

Fatima Omar is a leader in certified coach training for ambitious, spiritual women like you.

Claim your
Extraordinary
self with lucrative, spiritually-riched
CERTIFIED
Coach Training

If you desire to create a lucrative + spiritual coaching business that you are 100% in love with (without putting any time into creating coaching content from scratch), then our certified coach trainings are definitely for you.

Together, let's do this.

BE A COACH MASTERCLASS TRAINING
MillionStarsMasterClass.com

Free Coach Training
3 STEPS TO GET STARTED AS A SPIRITUAL BUSINESS COACH FOR WOMEN ENTREPENEURS

Transform Your Past, Pain and Skills into

Purpose, Power and Profit

SAVE YOUR SEAT
MillionStarsMasterClass.com

Notes:

Notes: ✍

OTHER BOOKS BY
Fatima Omar Khamissa & Platinum Publishing

Brilliance: Profiles of Extraordinary Innovators,
Experts & Leaders

Healing : Health and wellness industry experts share their insider
secrets, experience and advice on healing

#MortgageDonts by Athena Constantinou

The Second Wife by Shirin Ariff

Million Stars Changing Lives, Finding Freedom
and Building Personal Power

How to be a Muslim Woman,
Divorced and Totally Confident

From Ex to Extraordinary –
How to Make Your Divorce A Springboard for Excellence

Fearless Faith

50 Ways to Brand Yourself Online for Free

What is Verbal Abuse

To contact Fatima and her team at Platinum Publishing
Send an email to info@FatimaOmarKhamissa.com

www.ingramcontent.com/pod-product-compliance
Lightning Source LLC
Chambersburg PA
CBHW022143050726
47590CB00002B/563